REDEEMING THE TIME

Redeeming the Time

JAMES V. SCHALL, S.J.

SHEED AND WARD : NEW YORK

FOR My Sisters and Brothers
Mary Jo, Jeanne Louise, Norma Jeanne
John Joseph, Jerome Timothy

ACKNOWLEDGMENT

The author wishes to thank the editors of *America*, *The Catholic World*, *The Commonweal*, *The Month*, *Religion in Life*, *The Thomist*, *Thought*, and *Worship* for permission to adapt material which first appeared in their pages.

Contents

REDEEMING THE TIME

Introduction

The Christian has a most profound reason for appreciating Aristotle's fundamental insight that man is a being whose nature it is to live in the polis. This reason is that the one God of the Christian faith contains three different persons who are not reducible to one another. For the Christian, there must be a relation between these two truths. It does not seem to him to be a mere accident that the perfection of the life of God reveals a union of persons, just as the perfection of man himself seems to be also a union of persons. Moreover, the Christian is just that, a Christian; that is, he is a believer in the uniqueness of Christ, both as God and as man. Now this aspect of Christianity is also directly pertinent to man's sociality, for it affirms that God did not disdain or shun the reality of man's earthly life, which is social. Again, there is for man a direct connection with God through the world because the Word became flesh in it.

Yet the world and its realities have not always been easy for Christians to accept. This is a truth especially relevant today, when more perhaps than ever before the world seems

striving to become one society—one society which oftentimes believes that it is self-created and contains its destiny
within itself. Christianity has suffered acutely, because of its
very nature it is tempted to go to extremes in the stress it
places on God, on the one hand, and man in the world on
the other. Thus it finds itself sympathetic to all movements
which strive to exalt the dignity of man and at the same time
to those which see the greatness of God exalted above all
worldly things. But this capacity of Christianity is viewed
with considerable suspicion, because it is not easy to understand the delicate balance between God and the world implied
by the incarnation of the Son of Man.

The fact is, however, that some overall effort to see again
the true implications of Christianity in the vast complexities
of the society of men is of real value at this time. Certainly,
the achievement of Vatican II makes this attempt easier today.
The work of the Council is fundamental in trying to understand how Christianity looks at the values of the worldly
society. But over and above the public work of the Council
it remains the task of Christians to develop the wider implications of the fundamental beliefs of the Christian faith and
make them concrete in a personal, meaningful way. This
effort yields rather unexpected results. For considering the
unique aspects of Christianity as they apply to the society
of men in the world serves to reaffirm their permanent values,
and to reaffirm them—surprisingly, when one thinks of it—
as directly pertinent to the problems one must deal with if
one is to live in awareness of the issues of our times. If we
can briefly characterize the purpose of this book, then, it is

to think through the issues of modern society and of the modern world in the light of the abiding Christian truths which seem like a direct response to the questions raised by the realities of modern society.

1

Man in This World: God Calls Man As He Is

The world that man knows is both glorious and dark. It is a world which begets and supports him; it is a world which seems somehow designed for him to dwell in. In the history of Christianity, the task of God in the world had been accomplished when man accepted God's plan; God has chosen to work with man as he is. Yet the world has its obscurities, its sins, its evil, its sufferings, and its despair. If we are to discover how God works in the world and what it is that is unique about man, we must see that God's call is addressed to man in the very world which he has made within and around himself; these concrete earthly surroundings are not a context from which God plans to transfer him, miraculously removing him from the anguish of sin, death, suffering, and evil. It is, of course, the fundamental responsibility of the Christian to live in the hope, the belief, that he can be loyal to himself and to his neighbor while remaining loyal to God. But whatever the world which man finally creates for himself is like, even should it be a vast prison, he will discover that it is precisely in this man-made world that he will experience God's call for him. Man is redeemed from the point where

God finds him. And God finds him where and as he is in the world.

We can undoubtedly see the real context of man as we know him today most easily in our literature about him; what a generation writes about itself serves to indicate what man thinks himself to be. Here in a graphic sense, we can see the man with whom our Christian theology must deal.

But the interchange between Christian thought and literature is not always an easy one. Cultural and intellectual traditions have tended to separate formal theology and literature into diverse, often opposing, mutually deaf groups. Theology has been popularly considered as an "abstract," generally vague discipline, a thought pattern that has usually been regarded as merely irrelevant or uninteresting. Literature, on the other hand, is felt to penetrate into the concrete, into lived situations. It sees the human reality, which theology speaks of in remote terms, in the vivid lives and loves of the vast complexity of men who are born and who die. "The presence of grace," to employ J. F. Powers' term, is seen to be visible, down-to-earth, incarnated in lives of incredible disarray and ambiguity. The person attuned to religious questions today cannot but be struck by the vitality and reality of the theological overtones in current literature, cinema, theater, and art. In contrast with his somewhat methodological and categorical way of treating human problems, a theologian is constantly surprised to discover that much of the very best probing about human reality appears in novels, films, poems, paintings, and plays—works written by a wide variety of men and women from an amazing variety of viewpoints. What is even more astonishing is the frequency with which literary issues are also theological ones, not professedly or even consciously, but theological none the less. The problems of morality, evil, God, sin, salvation, suffering, and death are quite as much present in the novel, the play, the film, and on the stage as in the exegesis of the biblical scholar or in the thesis of the dogmatic theologian.

Probably even on theological grounds we should not be surprised at this. Too often we are superficially inclined to associate theology with the moralistic, the pietistic, the immaterial and superfluous aspects of life, while we turn to literature to contemplate what actually does happen around us. Yet if we begin to take theology more seriously, which indeed we seem to be doing, we discover a remarkable correlation between the man theology describes—in Scripture, in theological reflections, in basic dogmas—and the man who stumbles and gropes his way through the pages of our literature.

The reason we have perhaps failed to note this correlation before is that we have stressed the ascetical and moral aspects of theology in our attempt to understand the man of today, whereas we should rather have been looking in the direction of dogma and Scripture. In his famous book *Christian Spirituality*, Pourrat made a thoughtful comment with regard to the Gnostics which is relevant here: "Error somehow rarely fails to lead to libertinage."[1] The reason this observation is significant is that it cautions us, when we look at the astonishing outburst of vice and degradation described in so much of our literature, not to conclude immediately that a moral problem is primarily at issue—that is, a problem merely of doing the "right things." Back of the effort and energy to do these "right things" is the order of reality or lack of it which makes the living of the moral life possible or worthwhile. G. L. Prestige remarked in his study *God in Patristic Thought* that "Christian morality does not appear to survive for many generations after the loss of Christian dynamic faith."[2] In other words, when there is confusion in the order of dogma and intellect, it will be almost impossible to preserve morality. Conversely, as we shall suggest, when the moral confusion and disorder resulting from dogmatic difficulties has run its course, when there is little left to try, man's path back to an ordered universe will almost always grow naturally out of his attempt to feel and do the "right thing."

Nevertheless what we are witnessing today in all our literary and artistic endeavors is not primarily an intellectual investigation of the structure of reality—we have not arrived at this point yet, though this is basic and is present in part—but a constant probing and a growing honesty about what man by himself has wrought. The classical rebellions with which man has experimented in literature and life are rapidly exhausting themselves, disappearing, now that the "last frontier" of sex is successfully breached. What is left is no longer man full of the zest of revolutionary expectations about some millennium that will automatically arise after the next barricade is smashed, but merely naked man by himself, wondering how it is possible, now that the walls are down, that he still cannot save himself; wondering finally from whence his own salvation ultimately might arise. And this wonder is no longer directed to political, economic, or evolutionary destinies—these have been effectively undermined by the realities of our times—but rather to the personal milieu being born out of an accumulated literary tradition which has carried the burden of exhausting every avenue to redemption conceivable in man's own terms.[3] This development, of course, is not yet complete. Indeed, it is at a crossroads; but we can begin to observe its obscure outlines. Theologically, they are full of hope.

THE MEMORY OF ORDER

The scope and importance of this problem of the meaning of redemption in man's world can best be appreciated by looking at three passages from the literature of the last century, one from Shelley, one from Dostoyevsky, and one from Tolstoy. What we wish to suggest here is that we shall find in the nineteenth century a vision of order, or at least the hope of one, in which there is some definable relation between a structure of reality, not always obviously Christian, and the resolution of the basic human issues under consideration. What we perceive especially is a method of reducing death and suffering in particular to intelligible, believable dimensions. E. M. Forster perceived the feeling very well: "Death destroys a man, but the idea of death saves him—that is the best account of it that has yet been given."[4]

The atmosphere of progress and enthusiasm at this time in Western history made it easy to believe that mankind was on the verge of a fantastic breakthrough in which all sorrows would soon cease through human effort. Shelley expressed this in the final chorus of "Hellas":

> Oh, cease! must hate and death return?
> Cease! must men kill and die?

> Cease! drain not to its dregs the urn
> Of bitter prophecy!
> The world is weary of the past,
> Oh, might it die or rest at last!

We note here a profound impatience with the world as it is;
indeed, we note a rejection of what has gone before. The
hate, the suffering, and the killing are rejected outright. Let
the world die before such bitter realities are permitted to continue! But the context here is really more of hope, for there
is a hint, a suggestion, that mankind will not die but will turn
from its weary past. We feel here the demand for universal
redemption, or perhaps not a redemption so much as a recreation that would eradicate the context of sin and suffering
in which men are confined. This is really a post-Christian
utopia couched in pre-Christian terms, the willingness to
abandon men if they do not reform their environment, the
ultimate expression of the refusal to accept the human
condition.

In contrast with Shelley's lament is a brief conversation in
Dostoyevsky's *The Brothers Karamazov* between the aged
ascetic, Father Zossima, and Madame Hohlakov, a young and
attractive widow, during which she desperately confesses to
him that she has lost her faith. She pleads with him to instruct
her, to give her some "proof" which will enable her to believe.
Father Zossima replies patiently that there are no such proofs;
she can only reestablish what she has lost "by the experience
of active love. Strive to love your neighbor actively and in-
defatigably. In so far as you advance in love, you will grow

surer of the reality of God and the immortality of your soul."[5] What is of importance in this episode is the cause of the woman's anguish, namely, the question of life beyond the grave. Anxiety has forced her to reexamine her faith, and Father Zossima, following a classic formula of Augustine's, explains to her that active love of her neighbor as he really is—not a love of abstract humanity, to which she, like many other devout persons, was inclined—was the one sure way to love and belief in God and to the assurance of the future life. Dostoyevsky's development clearly relies on an order of spiritual reality in which there are answers to the ills and paradoxes of the human situation. Man does not regain his faith by looking into himself, but by turning outward to his neighbor and upward to God. In this context, we see a common acceptance of the general Christian framework according to which man can face without despair the vicissitudes of humanity's sin and faithlessness.

Just before Tolstoy's Anna Karenina cast herself to her tragic death on the rails, she sat pondering a snatch of conversation she had overheard on the train: "That's what reason is given man for, to escape from what worries him." "To escape from what worries him," Anna repeated in her thoughts. "Yes, I'm very much worried, and that's what reason was given me for, to escape. . . . Why not put the light out when there's nothing more to look at, when it's sickening to look at it at all? But how? Why did the conductor run along the footboard, why are they shrieking, those young men in that train? Why are they talking, why are they laughing? It's falsehood, all lying, all humbug, all evil."[6] Her decision to commit suicide had already corroded her perceptions; the ordinary scenes of life about her lost all their reality; already she was cut off from life.

In this same novel the young husband Levin, suffering traumatic effects from the death of his brother, is also tempted to suicide. He had come to the realization that "for every man, and himself too, there was nothing in store but suffering and death, and eternal oblivion."[7] It seemed to him that he must either shoot himself or reinterpret his life in such a way as to find meaning and goodness in it. But he did not do either. He went on living; he carried on with his daily life, married, and had considerable happiness when he was not preoccupied with his central problem about the meaning of life. After two years, he was suddenly given insight into his situation which brought him relief from anxiety. He realized that his happiness had come from living according to the spiritual truths in which he had been nurtured, accepting and not thinking about them. He saw that the answer to his perplexities was somehow given in the context of his own living. "The answer has been given me by life itself, in my knowledge of what is right and what is wrong. And that knowledge I did not arrive at in any way, it was given to me as to all men, *given*, because I could never have learned it from anywhere."[8] He could never have gathered by means of the faculty of reason the essential truth that life had taught him, for "loving one's neighbor, reason could never discover, because it's unreasonable."[9]

Tolstoy and Dostoyevsky differ from Shelley in their capacity for seizing the real in the context of man's sufferings and delusions and recognizing that man can reach redemption through them; yet all three share the vision of an order of brotherhood somehow lying behind and reducing to unity man's experience of life.

THE RISE OF REBELLION

If we look at literature and art in the twentieth century, we cannot but be struck at the role which rebellion has played in it. This is, in part, of course, the product of the cycle of generations, the younger generation establishing itself in autonomy by breaking with its immediate predecessor. There is also the need for novelty and originality—what was said before cannot simply be repeated. Nevertheless, it seems valid to maintain that we have witnessed an experiment in rebellion in our literature that has been a progressive quest of being itself in its portrayal of men who seek to affirm themselves by questioning and attacking the accepted standards of religion, politics, morals, and economics. Mr. Joseph Hayes has vividly described this mood as it manifests itself in the present-day theater:

In a time when the ever-present negative forces of a perilously balanced universe can finally win in a total way, the theater presents us with a picture of man's hopelessness, lack of significance or value under an empty, scowling sky, his self-deluded stupidity, cupidity, contemptible puniness—his utter worthlessness. . . . Their [the writers'] protest, if any, seems to be against the human condition as such—a sort of drawn-out egoistic whine in which they themselves seem to take . . . personal satisfaction. . . .[10]

Thus from the "ash-can" school of American art in the early 1900's, to novels of disgust produced by World War I, to the Depression plots depicting the alienation of man from the land, from *Main Street* to *1984*, we have castigated ourselves and our morals in the constant hope of discovering some key to personal and corporate salvation, some means, wholly new and effective, of escaping from the miasma of the existing world.[11]

In the course of all this, rebellions have resulted in new rebellions, and so we have a perennial phenomenon of evil and tragedy as the life of society more and more runs counter to all conventional norms. But ironically, we wish to suggest here, this process has begun to produce, out of its own dynamism, another effect: man is being forced to take another look at real life, a look at what rebellion has wrought. And this reexamination has taken an unexpected turn. Out of its own exigencies it has been yielded a glimpse of the truth in Zossima's and Levin's outlook: that the need for redemption is real; that it comes from outside ourselves and is related to other persons; that essentially it involves loving and is bound up with our sufferings and limitations themselves. In short, it rises out of the context of life itself, out of the needs of man in this world.

The recognition of the need for salvation and the reality of it is arising as the natural product of man's rebellion. This is especially true of the man who is exhausted and confused, having run the gamut of rebellion, when he is brought to the sorrowful realization of the harm done to the innocent through his deviations. He has rejected all moral standards as forms of alienation, only to discover belatedly the love and kindness and humanity retained in the poorest, most ordinary, most conventional lives. Man again appears as a creature who has learned, in Marquand's phrase, "that freedom of choice is limited," that man must accept the imperfections of humanity if he is to appreciate and love what has been given to him in the world.[12] Indeed, we only have an imperfect world and imperfect men dwelling in it. If we are not to love these, if we cannot find the divine somehow within the context of the imperfect, then as finite humans we cannot find love or God at all.

The most important philosophical objection to God's existence is founded on the existence of evil and suffering, and indeed the greatest paradox concerning the Christian God is his permission of suffering and evil while he remains the omnipotent God of love. Man's true freedom and nobility consist in living in an imperfect world without denying God because of this evil, limitation, and suffering. Living his life in such circumstances reveals the meaning which these realities have for him. Paul Claudel, perhaps more than any other, has reminded us of what is at stake here:

Dona Prouheze: Love without the sacrament, is it not sin?
The Guardian Angel: Even sin! Sin also serves.
Dona Prouheze: So it was good that he loved me?
The Guardian Angel: It was good that you taught him longing.[13]

The solution of this problem does not mean any reduction of God's power or his mercy. What finally makes man a Christian is that he can perform this seemingly impossible balancing act between the belief in God's existence and the recognition

of the sin and evil in the world because the Word was made
flesh and dwelt amongst us, because God's plan for us did
not involve taking us out of the actual world in which we
find ourselves. The Christian approach to the world must
finally be based on the quiet words with which John begins
the narrative of the Last Supper: "He had always loved those
who were his in the world. . . ." (John 13:1) Those who were
his were weak, they were sinners, they were ordinary. All
sanity begins with recalling this.

Lord of the Flies has recently reminded us that evil is
somehow present in human nature and, further, that it is not
necessarily or even primarily connected with sex, as a cursory
reading of much of modern literature and drama might seem
to suggest. Yet if evil is in the atmosphere, so to speak, its
reality is nevertheless found at the core of literature not so
much because it is present as because its presence somehow
involves man immediately with the question of God. The
Lord of the Flies simply records that evil is present among us;
it makes no further comment. Joseph Heller, in his novel
Catch 22, however, begins to come to grips with its implications when the novel's somewhat improbable hero protests:

> Good God! how much reverence can you have for a supreme
> being who finds it necessary to include such phenomena as phlegm
> and tooth decay in his divine system of creation? What in the
> world was running through that warped, evil, scatological mind of
> his when he robbed old people of the power to control their bowel
> movements? Why in the world did he create pain?[14]

This is the rebellion against God because of the existence of
pain and evil. Its thesis is, obviously, that God could not allow

such a thing and still be God. There is no real room for redemption in this view, however, because of the implicit denial that God and pain could both somehow exist simultaneously. But this line of protest, reproduced in a thousand different forms in modern literature, is really a hopeless one. For if we will not admit the possibility of God and evil both being present in the same universe, only two alternatives remain. Either God does not exist, or evil (the same argument holds for pain) is something that can be fully removed by human effort. But if God does not exist, evil nevertheless remains and the problem is unsolved. And we are beginning to see with certainty that man can only remove some of the evil and suffering among us. Thus the second alternative vanishes also. Only despair seems left. But despair attacks freedom, and freedom is what establishes man in the first place as an autonomous person.

Most literature today is not at the point where it sees clearly that the dilemma of evil, suffering, and God can only be resolved by recognizing the presence of all these in the world. Theology has carefully attempted to discuss the problem of evil in such a manner as to show that God could allow evil but still not be its cause. In theology, evil is attributed first to the choice of man, then, in a secondary sense, to the working out of natural laws—such as that the death of the rabbit is the life of the wolf. But literature has refused to accept what it regards as a pat solution. Many writers have remained convinced that God is really responsible, even if pain and evil are only things he merely permits. From them the implication remains that he cannot really be God. The notion that evil is a correlative of freedom in a creature and therefore, in a very real sense, a sign of man's exaltation by God, not of God's lack of concern for him, has never been adequately considered.

THE SENSE OF REDEMPTION

Nevertheless, the alternatives to God, namely, either despair or total reliance on human achievement, have both proved illusory. They have not answered the question. We can see in Clifford Odets' play with the significant title *Paradise Lost* just how powerful the hope of some ultimate achievement is in man, while at the same time reminding ourselves how little likelihood there is that men can any longer believe in such naive optimism:

Everywhere now men are rising from their sleep. Men, men are understanding the bitter black total of their lives. Their whispers are growing to shouts! They become an ocean of understanding! No man fights alone. Oh, if you could only see with me the greatness of men. I tremble like a bride to see the time when they'll use it. My darling, we must have only one regret—that life is so short! That we must die so soon. Yes, I want to see that new world. I want to kiss all the future men and women. What is this talk of bankrupts, failures, hatred? . . . They won't know what that means. Oh, yes, I'll tell you the whole world is for men to possess. Heartbreak and terror are not the heritage of mankind! The world is beautiful. No fruit tree wears a lock and key. Men will sing as they work, men will love. Oh, darling, the world is in its morning . . . and no man fights alone.[15]

All the hopes of a paradise on earth are here; yet it is unreal, somehow inhuman, to forget the realities which in fact sur-

must we make such a thing of loneliness when it is the final condition of us all?"[21] Loneliness, however, is not a state of rest. It is conducive to listening, to expectation. Hannah, in *The Night of the Iguana*, makes a remark that tends in a direction in which the gap between loneliness, expectation, and the need of outside help can be bridged: "We all wind up with something or with someone, and if it's someone instead of just something, we're lucky, perhaps unusually lucky."[22]

The development of the idea of redemption in modern literature has, then, brought us to the point at which we can recognize that suffering and evil are going to be present no matter what form of rebellion we might conceive. Even more, there is often the hint we have seen in *The Satin Slipper* that "even sin serves," the notion Christians acquire from the Magdalene that sin can become the basis of redemption. Something of this can be felt in Jack Kerouac's *On the Road*: "I suddenly realized that Dean, by virtue of his enormous series of sins, was becoming the Idiot, the Imbecile, the saint of the lot."[23] Further, the existence of sin and evil is a spiritual problem with which man must grapple in his relationship between God and the world. This experience of living in such a world somehow excites notions and feelings of expectation—the *Waiting for Godot*—in the very depths of the men who feel guilt and loneliness most deeply and acutely. And, finally, it is clear that the beginnings of some redemptive experience have to do with other mortals, other persons,

The basic step in the further evolution of this concept was taken by Samuel and Lee and the Chinese scholars in *East of Eden* when they pursued exegesis far enough to discover that the issue about sin is one of choice—"thou mayest rule

over sin." "Thou mayest—that gives a choice. It might be the
most important word in the world. That says the way is open.
That throws it right back on a man. . . . 'Thou mayest'! Why,
that makes a man great, that gives him stature with the gods,
for in his weakness and his filth and his murder of his brother
he has still the great choice."[24] This is the initial realization
that man really does have some power of choice, some mo-
bility, with regard to his weakness and filth. God and evil are
not just absolutes struggling against each other in some
Manichean sense (as sometimes seems to be the case even in
Faulkner), two hostile forces outside man opposed to each
other; rather they are opposing presences within man himself.

With the recognition of our freedom even in the face of
sin must come the honest acceptance of what one is. A concept of redemption requires both these as initial stages. This is
the importance of Biff and Willy Loman. The delusions must
finally yield to reality, all of them. Biff confesses to his father:

> I am not a leader of men, Willy, and neither are you. You were
> never anything but a hard-working drummer who landed in the
> ash can like all the rest of them! I'm one dollar an hour Willy!
> I tried seven states and couldn't raise it. A buck an hour! . . .
> I'm not bringing home any prizes any more, and you're going to
> stop waiting for me to bring them home! . . . Pop, I'm nothing!
> I'm nothing, Pop. Can't you understand that? There's no spite
> in it any more. I'm just what I am, that's all.[25]

The beginning of any redemptive situation involves freedom and honesty, a freedom that combines with honesty to

see the real guilt and anguish that man has caused so that he can at last act upon it.

Beyond this, modern literature has taken one further halting but significant step. MacLeish's *J. B.*, it seems to me, begins it. When we at last come to recognize the human situation—our expectations, our freedom, our finiteness, our guilt—when we at last face up to the fact that our traditional supports have crumbled, there is still the spark of human love silently challenging the darkness.

> The candles in the churches are out.
> The lights have gone out in the sky.
> Blow on the coal of the heart
> And we'll see by and by.[26]

But the concept of blowing on the coal of the heart leaves us pretty much in the realm of abstractions, and for most moderns love is too often an abstraction. This is a weakness, for love needs human incarnation before it is real. J. D. Salinger, perhaps more than any other contemporary writer, has grasped this. And the significant thing is that this insight into the need to make our salvific love incarnate is not primarily erotic. Being with Phoebe in *Catcher in the Rye*, with Esmé, Sybil and several other small children in the *Short Stories*, Salinger becomes intuitively aware of the importance to man of a love outside himself, based on none of his instinctual needs but wholly in the order of gift. This is typified for him by the wonder of little girls. The incident of Zooey looking out the window at an eight-year-old down below, playing hide-and-seek with her little dachshund—the child's affec-

tionate delight when the confused mutt manages to find her—
is a case in point. Looking on this scene with something akin
to pure contemplation, Zooey finally murmurs: "God dammit
there are nice things in the world—and I mean nice things.
We're all such morons to get sidetracked, always, always
referring every goddam thing that happens right back to our
lousy little egos."[27]

None the less, if salvation is found in "otherness," it still
must come to grips with suffering, evil, and God. The statement is Faulkner's:

Stevens: The salvation of the world is in man's suffering. Is that
it?

Nancy: Yes, sir.

Temple: But why must it be suffering? . . . What kind of God
is it that has to blackmail His customers with the whole
world's grief and ruin?

Stevens: You have got to sin, too?

Nancy: You ain't got to. You can't help it. And He knows that.
But you can suffer. And He knows that too. He don't
tell you not to sin, he just asks you not to. He don't
tell you to suffer. But He gives you the chance. He
gives you the best He can think of, that you are capable
of doing. And He will save you.[28]

Obviously, the redemptive theme is very much present here.
Redemption takes place within the world as it is, the world
of pain and suffering. Children suffer; they are, as Nancy
says, our responsibility. Salvation is not something belonging
to another world, or something achieved for the world in a

past generation. It is right among men now in their ordinary lives. Faulkner's insight is very moving here; blind belief is for him the only assurance we have of the world's making sense.

Cass, in William Styron's *Set This House on Fire*, suddenly asks the final question that must be raised about redemption: "How will I ever forgive myself for all the things I've done?"[29] In his despair, he has seriously considered doing away with his wife and children: "It would be easy. But right then I heard Luigi's voice, adamant and outraged . . . 'Tu pecchi nell'avere tanto senso di colpa!' You sin in this guilt of yours! You sin in your guilt!"[30] Cass too faced the "thou mayest" of Samuel and Lee. Sin can be conquered. But how? The recognition of guilt is not enough, nor does the "you just got to believe" of Nancy in *Requiem* seem adequate of itself; it too inchoate, lacking the concrete hold which J. B. and Zooey have on the fact that salvation somehow lies not just in suffering but in the love of others. Styron's novel finally reaches a kind of resolution of this problem of guilt. But what is attained is not a real faith in which there is a balancing of suffering and joy—a resurrection. Rather it is limited to making a choice of facing and accepting the rest of the days of one's life:

But to be truthful, you see, I can only tell you this: that as for being and nothingness, the only thing I did know was that to choose between them was simply to choose being, not for the sake of being, or even the love of being, much less the desire to be forever—but in the hope of being what I could be for a time. This would be an ecstasy. God knows, it would.[31]

This, surely, is a statement of the present position of the
redemption theme in current literary thought. It accepts our
concrete life—that life which remains to man after his guilt,
rebellion, and fall—as somehow salvific, something worthwhile, something out of which the sins of the past can be
redeemed by suffering and love. In a sense, the whole structure of redemption is here, with the exception of the stage
at which Styron stops short—namely, the resurrection. But
only in the light of the resurrection can redemption be seen
fully as a gift of God. Boris Pasternak has seen this issue:
". . . art has two constant, unending concerns: it always medi-
tates on death and thus always creates life. All great genuine
art resembles and continues the Revelation of St. John."[32] In
the end, as Doctor Zhivago reflected, redemption is not redemption until the whole of life with all its limitations and
sufferings is transfigured and transformed; until these human
realities and the experience of them which runs through every
page of modern literature are at last also saved and redeemed;
until the Revelation of St. John is an eternal reality.

THE HOPE OF ORDER

There is a mystery here of the profoundest import. Why is
it that the man reflected in our literature with all its honesty
and frankness can pass, through rebellion and degradation, to
the recognition of his need of active love and of his inability
to save himself, yet, with all this somehow present in his
literary experience, be left not knowing where to turn? He
seems to end up alone with himself. The following passage
of Scott Fitzgerald's is a fair summary of the problem:

Amory, sorry for them, was still not sorry for himself—art, politics, religion, whatever his medium should be, he knew he was safe now, free from all hysteria—he would accept what was acceptable, roam, grow, rebel, sleep deep through many nights.

There was no God in his heart, he knew, his ideas were still in riot; there was even the pain of memory; the regret for his lost youth—yet the waters of disillusionment had left a deposit on his soul, responsibility and a love of life, the faint stirring of old ambitions and unrealized dreams. But—oh, Rosalind, Rosalind!

"It's all a poor substitute at best," he said sadly.

And he could not tell why the struggle was worth while, why he had determined to use to the utmost himself and his heritage from the personalities he had possessed. . . . He stretched out his arms to the crystalline, radiant sky.

"I know myself," he cried, "but that is all."[33]

Here is all the hope and anguish of self-knowledge combined with the intuitive certainty that it is not enough. This is, perhaps, the evidence from man's side of the theological doctrine that the initiation of the movement towards salvation does not belong primarily to man but comes from the depths of the divinity.

When we try to ascertain the meaning of this quest from man's side, we, as Christians, see that the path we must follow lies outside ourselves. In the final analysis, we are being saved, we are not saving ourselves. In the novel *Kristin Lavransdatter*, all these strands of thought about salvation which can be traced through modern literature are brought together in a passage of great power recording the thoughts of Kristin at the approach of death:

It seemed to her to be a mystery that she could not fathom, but which she knew most surely none the less, that God held her fast in a covenant made for her without her knowledge by a love poured out upon her richly—and in spite of all her self-will, in spite of her heavy earth-bound spirit, somewhat of his love had become part of her. . . . A handmaiden of God she had been—a wayward, unruly servant . . . slothful and negligent . . . but little constant in her deeds—yet had he held her fast in his service. . . . A mark had been set secretly on her showing that she was his handmaid, owned by the Lord and King who was now coming, borne by the priest's anointed hands, to give her freedom and salvation.[34]

The theme of redemption in modern literature and art, then, is at the crossroads in its development. If we regard this whole trend as a synthesis emerging dialectically, we cannot but be impressed by the way it has developed almost out of its own dynamism. What causes the human mind to act is almost always some series of problems or contradictions producing a dichotomy which it is forced to resolve. We have found the themes of degradation, rebellion, progress, love, selflessness, suffering, and salvation everywhere present in modern literature. We have seen a consistent growth in awareness of the need for redemption and in the need to find it in the very context of human life. This awareness somehow includes the worst aspects of life as well as the best. It confronts life and death with a presentiment that somehow there is an order outside our life and within it in which all of these seeming contradictions and paradoxes are summed up and reconciled.

It is evident that few see, as Sigrid Undset's Kristin did,

that salvation in any ultimate sense is God's as well as one's own doing, since the evils that we cause, our sufferings and our death, can finally be redeemed only if we can hope for eternal life as a gift from the outside which is nevertheless at work within the living context of our personal histories. But in the absence of this insight the theme of redemption in modern literature has reached a climax in its own order. It must either turn, with Nancy in *Requiem,* in some sense towards God as the source of redemption or come, sooner or later, face to face with the fact that the natural beginnings of redemption as depicted in Styron, MacLeish, or Salinger, which depend for their motives on human love between persons, leave the problems of death and suffering and love still unresolved; hence these incipient hopes can soon turn back into despair.

The theme of natural, personal redemption which we have been reviewing involves a very true and powerful grasp of human reality. It is a motif that has grown out of the very limitations of human experience. Yet, by the questions it raises, it forces us as Christians to pursue the theme of redemption to its ultimate ground. Man is again confronted with the "thou mayest," and there is no certainty how he will choose. But if he does decide to open himself to the implications of redemption in its fullest sense, to the real meaning of man in the world, he must be prepared to listen, to ask himself whether there really is an order to which he belongs, whether he really has a vocation in the world.

The Christian is primarily concerned with the redemption of the historical, actual man whom it is the role of our literature to describe; real men created in this universe by a loving

God. The Christian's anguish and hope must be the anguish and hope of our race. Christians today are prepared to ask ultimate questions proper to mankind: What is our destiny? Can we reach eternal life? Is God in our midst? Does the world belong to us? What is God's role?[35] In literature the focus in which these problems are seen may differ from that of life. Often art presents things more vividly, more concretely, to us. Yet the writer or artist cannot hope for more than other men hope for, and what man hopes for in a way defines what he is. And the question of what man is, is a preoccupation common to us all. In the end, we are concerned with order, with some principle that separates us or brings us together; which allows us to fall back into nothingness or transforms us and our all too unimpressive yet somehow noble lives by drawing them into the presence of grace, into the redemption of ourselves and our brothers.

NOTES

1. P. Pourrat, *Christian Spirituality*, tr. S. P. Jacques (London: Burns, Oates and Washbourne, 1924), Vol. I, p. 66.

2. G. L. Prestige, *God in Patristic Thought* (London: S.P.C.K., 1952), p. xvi.

3. Cf. Edmund Fuller, *Man in Modern Fiction* (New York: Vintage, 1958).

4. E. M. Forster, *Howard's End* (New York: Vantage, 1958), p. 324.

5. F. Dostoyevsky, *The Brothers Karamazov*, tr. Constance Garnett (New York: Halcyon House, 1940), p. 63.

6. Leo Tolstoy, *Anna Karenina*, First Modern Library Edition, tr. Constance Garnett, edited and introduced by Leonard J. Kent and Nina Berberova (New York: Random House, 1965), p. 796.

7. *Ibid.*, p. 830.

8. *Ibid.*

9. *Ibid.*

10. Joseph Hayes, "Distorted Views of Life," *The New York Times*, August 14, 1963, p. 8.

11. The following passage from Archibald MacLeish's important essay presents the current climate of opinion: "The principal orientation of this later work . . . is briefly and, I think, brilliantly described by Susan Sontag . . . 'One of the primary features of literature (as of much activity in all the other arts) in our times is a chronic attachment to materials belonging to the realm of "extreme situations" —madness, crime, taboo sexual longings, drug addiction, emotional degradation, violent death. The motive or justification for this loyalty to extreme situations is obscure. It is felt that such situations are somehow "more true" than others; that an art immersed in such situations is "more serious" than other art, and finally, that only art that embraces the irrational and repellent, the violent and the outrageous, can make a valuable impact on the sluggish consciousness of the audience.'

"This, of course, is something more than a description of the writing of some of our best-known contemporaries: It is also, in its assumptions and implications—and in some of its explicit statements—an account of the beliefs, particularly the beliefs about mankind, on which their writing is founded and which, as serious work of art, it exists to express. To say that the literature of 'extreme situations'—of 'madness, crime, taboo sexual longings, drug addiction, emotional degradation, violent death'—is felt by its authors to be 'more true' means, of course, more true to man, more true to that human truth which is the measure of all literary truth. To say that an art immersed in 'extreme situations' is felt by its creators to be 'more serious' means more humanly serious—more worthy of serious human attention. And to say that 'only art which embraces the irrational and repellent, the violent and the outrageous,' is felt to be capable of making a 'valuable impact on the sluggish consciences of the audience,' is to comment, in most explicit terms, on the opinions about mankind of the creators of this art." Archibald MacLeish, "There Was Something About the Twenties," *The Saturday Review*, December 31, 1966, p. 11.

Commenting on the recent San Francisco Film Festival, Mr. Sarel Eimerl has written: "The forces that since the Second World War have been sweeping novels and films down into the furnaces of hell in its various forms have now grown so overpowering that it seems pointless to struggle against them. Writers and directors alike appear to have been infected with a distorted narcissism that keeps them preoccupied with human ugliness and misery. One can only wait until the disease has run its course and the artists return to a healthier and more balanced view of the human condition. However, watching twenty-one art movies in eleven days concentrates a man's mind wonderfully, and the experience convinced me that the disease has reached a more advanced stage than I had supposed." Sarel Eimerl, "A Plea for the Vieille Vague," *The Reporter*, December 15, 1966, pp. 52–53.

12. John P. Marquand, *Point of No Return* (New York: Grosset and Dunlap, 1951), p. 526.

13. Paul Claudel, *The Satin Slipper* (New York: Sheed and Ward, 1937), p. 72.

14. Joseph Heller, *Catch 22* (New York: Dell, 1961), p. 184.

15. Clifford Odets, "Paradise Lost," *Six Plays by Clifford Odets* (New York: Modern Library, 1933), p. 229.

16. Robinson Jeffers, *The Selected Poetry of Robinson Jeffers* (New York: Random House, 1937), p. 575. "Where I?" from *Solstice and Other Poems* by Robinson Jeffers.

17. St. Augustine, *The City of God*, tr. G. G. Walsh et al. (Garden City, N.Y.: Image Books, 1952), p. 46.

18. John Updike, *Rabbit Run* (New York: Crest Books, p. 107).

19. Tennessee Williams, *The Fugitive Kind* (Orpheus Descending), (New York: Signet Books), p. 63. © 1955, 1958 by Tennessee Williams. Reprinted by permission of New Directions Publishing Corp.

20. Graham Greene, *The Quiet American* (New York: Viking, 1955), p. 78.

21. John O'Hara, *Sermons and Soda Water* (New York: Bantam), p. 214.

22. Tennessee Williams, *The Night of the Iguana* © 1961 by Two Rivers Enterprise, Inc. Reprinted by permission of New Directions Publishing Corporation.

23. Jack Kerouac, *On the Road* (New York: Signet, 1957), p. 160.

24. John Steinbeck, *East of Eden* (New York: Viking, 1952), p. 303.

25. Arthur Miller, *Death of a Salesman* (New York: Bantam, 1951), p. 144. Reprinted by permission of The Viking Press, Inc.

26. Archibald MacLeish, *J. B.* (Boston: Houghton Mifflin, 1956), p. 153.

27. J. D. Salinger, *Franny and Zooey* (Boston: Little, Brown, 1961), p. 151.

28. William Faulkner, *Sanctuary and Requiem for a Nun* (New York: Signet, 1951), pp. 331–332.

29. William Styron, *Set This House on Fire* (New York: Signet), p. 379. Reprinted with the permission of Random House, copyright 1960.

30. *Ibid.*, p. 466.

31. *Ibid.*, pp. 476–477.

32. Boris Pasternak, *Doctor Zhivago* (New York: Pantheon, 1958), p. 90.

33. F. Scott Fitzgerald, *This Side of Paradise* (New York: Scribner, 1920).

34. Sigrid Undset, *Kristin Lavransdatter* (New York: Knopf, 1937), pp. 1040–1041.

35. Cf. Vatican II, "The Church Today," *The Documents of Vatican II*, ed. W. Abbott (New York: Angelus, 1966), no. 10, p. 208. Excerpts from The Constitutions and Declarations of the Ecumenical Council are taken from *The Documents of Vatican II*, published by Guild Press, America Press, and Herder and Herder, and copyrighted 1966 by The America Press. Used by permission.

2

The Silence of God:
God Is on Man's Side

A feeling, then, a need for redemption exists among the men of our time, a fleeting suspicion that across their all too human lives, across their sins as well as their glories, there is something, someone who calls them. Yet, the indications seem to be, from our reflections on modern literature and drama, that modern man does not easily hear anything but his own voice in the pathways of time. He is likely to regard the believer as a rather quaint figure—somewhat consoling, perhaps, but nevertheless someone who is definitely far removed from the sphere of practical possibilities in which the thoughts and hopes of modern man function. For the Christian, therefore, the question immediately arises, Why is it so difficult, so agonizing, for his contemporaries in this world to hear the voice of God? Certainly the Christian can share the fear of death and suffering, he can participate in love and comradeship, he can hate sin and still not abandon the sinner along with everyone else. But in the end, why is it that everyone does not hear the same voice, the same call across the hard realities of life, across all the thresholds and contradictions that modern literature and life have shown us? This is the mystery.

For the Christian, God is the Lord of History. "I am the Alpha and the Omega, *the First and the Last,* the Beginning and the End." (Revelation 22:13) The will of God will be done. Yet God can be rejected by man. Hell is the rejection of God, the refusal to accept his life as one's personal destiny. God, on the other hand, can also be accepted by man. But what does it mean for man to accept God? This is no simple problem. For the subjective acceptance of God today does not always seem to mean the correlative acceptance of formal religion, or the immediate appreciation of those who are supposed to be God's representatives. Hypocrisy is always a present danger. Religion, in spite of its many efforts towards modernization, is still often accused of being irrelevant today. It often seems to have no important bearing on the things which interest man. The important issues of our time seem not to have religious roots—or, even more often, religious solutions. Does this mean that the call of God has been absent during these recent ages when it has appeared that all those having power in the world have set religion aside as untrue or insignificant? But if, on the contrary, God has been present in fact, what form has his presence taken? This is perhaps one of the crucial issues we face perpetually if we are to recognize the meaning of the destiny to which man is called.

Of all the temptations to which the religious mind is subjected, the most subtle, perhaps the most disturbing, is the impulse to demand of God a visible sign, a tangible, unmistakable proof that God is physically, as it were, on the side of religion.[1] Will you now establish the Kingdom of Israel?

(Cf. Acts 1:6) Thus, were we to have such visible signs, there would be no room for doubt or uncertainty; no area for conflict or controversy would arise to bother us. In exasperation, we are often in sympathy with the Prophet, when he asked of God, "Why do you look on while men are treacherous, and stay silent while the evil man swallows a better man than he?" (Habakkuk, 1:13) Yet this demand that God break the silence he seems to keep is often a desire to transform belief in God into a necessary, coerced conclusion. God is to be believed because man *must* believe, there is to be no choice whatsoever. The silence of God, however, as we shall see, is the other side of God's own creation of man as free, of the belief that the only worthy response man can give to God is a free response. Furthermore, if we look at it, the New Testament was very hard on the representatives of the formal religion of the time. The worst way to worship God was the way the scribes and Pharisees did. (Matthew 16:12) The approval of God broke through all expected norms, it was reserved for unlikely and disliked people like Matthew, the Samaritan, and the Magdalene. Each generation, it seems, confronts this problem of reading the signs of its times to see whether the silence of God does not, in fact, mean that it must find God in places where it least expects to find him.

Thus the perplexities of modern Christians are many, perhaps too many. God, they believe, is light. The light has shone in the world to disperse the darkness. God, they believe, is word. This word has spoken amongst us. There is need for listening, for noise and shouting, for answers and responses. Christians believe, with Chesterton, that the model of their destiny is the inn, not the cell. Unlike other believers,

Christians really have no word for God that means depth, or silence, or darkness. Their goal is always vision, their source is light, their way and life is word, their belief is through hearing.

God is light and presence in the world. But who hears him? Who indeed speaks for him? Surely the answer that many Christians would most spontaneously give to such a query would be that God speaks through his representatives, through the Church. Yet, as the Dutch theologian R. C. Kwant has warned, how carefully we must phrase what we say concerning this matter. "In the nineteenth century," he observes, "solicitous concern with the discredited social systems originated outside the Church and it took the Church a long time to give official sanction to the movement for reform."[2] *Rerum Novarum* came late in the Industrial Revolution, just as permission to teach in Rome that the earth travels around the sun came very late (1822) in the scientific revolution. Further, if we look at an institution like slavery, we can say with some justice that the Christian belief in the dignity of man was in part responsible for its mitigation and eventual abolition. But the recognized leaders in the modern phase of this fight, the men who actually did the effective work—men like Wilberforce, John Brown, and Lincoln—were for the most part religious men but not men of religion. And even religious men like the Spanish theologian Las Casas who were also men of religion often met their strongest opposition in their superiors, lay and ecclesiastical. There had been, before very recent years, no modern religious document to compare with the Emancipation Proclamation or the Declaration of Independence on the subject of human dignity and rights.

Moreover, if we examine the numerous topics so well treated in *Mater et Magistra, Pacem in Terris,* and *Populorum Progressio,* and in many of the decrees of Vatican II, we cannot but be impressed by the number of these steps toward reform, now approved, which were originally envisioned, or encouraged, or preserved, or championed by men and groups outside the formal Church—such diverse items as those concerning constitutionalism, human rights, liberty of conscience, vernacular in worship, freedom of speech, social insurance, foreign aid, scientific scripture studies, world government, procedural rights, respect for alien cultures, rights of minorities, the legitimacy of democracy and the right to political opposition, racial equality, population problems. The spirit breathes where it will. None the less, it is legitimate to say that any competent, objective study of the development of most of these subjects in modern times would reveal too little evidence that official religion has been the main cause of their acceptance and development: they are officially accepted now because they must be recognized to be parts of the human patrimony. To be sure, there have often been powerful religious influences, and here and there a man of religion will have made a vital contribution; but overall and for the most part, the men, parties, and organizations most responsible for these results in modern times have worked outside the ecclesiastical world. We must still, if we are honest with ourselves, allowing whatever we may to exaggeration or prejudice, feel uneasy before this phenomenon.

But the problem is even deeper than this. More and more in our time, we are seeing the Church accept belatedly, often hastily, notions of the public welfare, equality, spiritual freedom, and human dignity that have been commonplace in much of civil theory and society for a long time, notions that have been made real and effective by civil and societal, not ecclesial, powers. In one sense, it is most tempting to conclude with many contemporary thinkers that God is just a bit dead. It does seem rather unsettling when religion appears to be the last, or nearly the last, to accept publicly rights and duties commonly acknowledged by most men anyhow. Religious documents almost up till Vatican II have seemed so hesitant, so agonizingly slow, to admit the good in social and cultural movements wherever it might be found. Enthusiasm for mere negative criticism is almost impossible to maintain. The world, rightly or wrongly, expects religion to be a leader, not a follower.

Furthermore, the very manner in which religion has traditionally spoken to the world is no longer received with much sympathy. Concern about Church structure as seemingly out-of-date, as somehow an antiquated form of monarchy, is heard everywhere. These comments of a prominent layman are not untypical:

Years of anti-lay conditioning have left a certain distrust among many of the clergy. A climate prevails, too, in which monologues are the usual rectory fare and the pastor is wary of the curate-who-reads. The Church's vertical lines of authority aren't channeled for proper, open dialogue. You don't dialogue with an absolute monarch—and up until the present revolution that is what we have had. Many dioceses and parishes still operate on such lines.[3]

And this is not so much a problem of the nature of authority; rather, it is a question of the modes of exercising authority. Authority can be exercised like a Roman emperor or a commissar or an Indian chief. Modern democratic experience has learned much about the nature of authority in this sense, especially its realization that the subjects of authority are also mature and intelligent. There is a worried doubt, then, about ecclesiastical power when it seems to be exercised against man's human dignity. In a sense, the memories of the Inquisition and the Index, whatever the supposed justifications for these measures, have cast a shadow of suspicion over all churchly authorities. Professor Jerome Kerwin has underscored this problem:

But who judges the judge? Who says to religious authority that it must not trespass on man's freedom? Who shall convince it of sin when it, too, becomes organized tyranny? Who unmasks the hidden face of oppression that wears a holy countenance? Above all, who possesses the omnicompetency that permits him to draw with precision the line that separates the two powers?[4]

The actual political organs used by the Church in her day-to-day operations seem to the modern world modeled more closely on historic, absolute states than we are accustomed to admit. In brief, it is today no longer wise or even possible for the Church to operate with a political, external structure based in fact not on the New Testament, but on absolute states, and more particularly, on traditions which arose at a time in history when the Church did exercise temporal power.

Too little attention has been paid to the way in which the "power of the keys" has been facilely equated with the psychological and institutional forms proper not to the Church itself, but to a form of political life originating in fifteenth-to nineteenth-century Europe.[5]

It seems clearer today, as the Church itself is just beginning to face the problem of its own administrative reform, that the reason the Church has developed no adequate and proper legislative organs, no public traditions of "ecclesiastical" civil rights, no "independent" judiciary constantly asking Church government how closely it is conformed to the Gospel is not that such procedures and institutions would be somehow forbidden by Scripture or tradition—collegiality and the Synod of Bishops implies just the opposite, as does the ancient tradition of local election of bishops—but that the administrative political model that the papacy and episcopacy have followed lacked these structures for its own people in the civil order. How far such a model was from the ideal can be seen by recalling that even St. Thomas requires of his monarchic theory that it incorporate also legislative and judicial powers within its very structure precisely as an assurance that the monarch have an adequate awareness of what is happening in the society over which he rules.[6]

The Church in its institutions has tended to take as a model the absolute, administrative side of government, to the neglect of the critical and balancing influences of legislative and judicial powers. Its closest modern analogy is a federal-executive-bureaucratic administration lacking a congress and a judiciary.[7] It has been too uncritically accepted that such balancing organs would weaken or undermine the papacy or episcopacy. But as American experience especially has proved, quite the opposite is likely to be true. This is why the Synod of Bishops and the various consultative and procedural organizations being set up in the various dioceses augurs well for the Church. The one remaining area that most needs attention lies in the direction of the internationalization of the Church's highest organs. Some minimal steps have already been taken, but the model of the United Nations sets an ideal and hope for international administration which a Church claiming to be universal in fact cannot any longer ignore.

The papal authority, as Newman said, must consult the Church, he must know in truth what all the faithful believe and think at any given time. And a personage like a pope dare not rely solely on his own advisors and staff whom he has himself appointed or who look to him for their job security. Outside the actual Council, too little progress on this score has been made, though fortunately we see beginnings. In a sense, every executive from a president or corporation head to a pope faces the same problem of how to be able to test and check his own advisors. But it is particularly interesting to note that the theological foundations for such reforms in the direction of more adequate representation and organization have been in Scripture and in tradition all along, in the priesthood of the faithful, in charisms, in collegiality, in the episcopacy, in the notion that authority is service, in the witness of the whole Church. Can we not predict and hope today that the Church's organs of government will more and more at every level—parish, diocesan, and papal—according to their own proper modes, develop the external forms of free, responsible democratic structures more and more recognized by the teaching Church itself in recent years to be the tendencies of the natural law in social organizations? Grace still builds on nature, even when nature has proved to grace how complex it is. And yet, here again, it is extremely annoying to wonder why the Church could not have inaugurated these reforms herself; why, in the history of modern times, she could not have been the model and guide to such human reforms and not the belated follower, could not have been, like the monastic assemblies of the Middle Ages, a source on which the world could rely to learn how to rule and govern.

WORLD WITHOUT LOGOS

Right at this point, then, the problem of the silence of God is most acute for the modern Christian. For if so many of the movements for human dignity, equality, freedom, and rights in modern history and in contemporary society have been, in fact, led by and championed by men who are not Christians, who often are even hostile, uninfluenced by, or indifferent to Christianity, how can we seriously claim that God speaks through the Church—especially now when, as we have already said, we find the Church finally approving so many of these very things it hesitated so long about? Why is not the skeptic, who attributes none of these advances to a call from God, who openly claims that man must forge his own dignity for himself—why is he not, in the final analysis, right? Why attribute ultimately to God what plainly was the result of human effort and at times achieved in spite of clerical or religious opposition?

This is a problem that deserves more attention than it is

wont to receive. Gerhard Szczesny's indictment is not unusual:

Anyone who without bias looks over the last thousand years of Western history is forced to the conclusion that Western man, the more his character matured, as he tried to penetrate the world's pattern not only in a practical way but by systematic and interpretative thought, the more he came into irreconcilable conflict with the Christian point of view. The Christian churches themselves bear eloquent witness to this state of affairs. Time and time again they resisted and charged with heresy the great spirits of the Renaissance and the periods of Enlightenment.[8]

Earlier in this book we dealt with another type of reaction in the various forms of literature of this generation. There is not so much a spirit of accusing God of being absent as a disappointment that he cannot be heard, a despair at the difficulty in finding him. The questions are everywhere asked, Are you silent, O God? Where is your voice? We would believe, but we do not hear you. Perhaps you are in the midst of love? perhaps in despair? in abandonment? in doubt? in loneliness? in magic? in violence? in friendship? Yet we are not sure we really hear you, the response seems only to be silence. Make us sure, make us hear. These brief lines from Archibald MacLeish's powerful *An Epistle Buried in the Earth* reveal such perplexities:

Also none among us has seen God
(. . . We have thought often
The flaws of sun in the late and driving weather
Pointed to one tree but it was not so)

As for the nights I warn you the nights are dangerous
The wind changes at night and the dreams come.[9]

To brooding and questioning of this kind about the silence
of God in the face of human tragedy, human doubt, and
human love, it has been tempting to answer that Well, of
course, such things are not the responsibility of Christians.
The persecuted Jews during Hitler's time were not members
of the Church; slavery was mostly economic and social; inte-
gration must follow state laws; social justice and civil rights
belong to the order of politics; liberty of conscience refers
primarily to the "truth," to believers. The role of the Church
is to concern itself with the real life of man, with personal
salvation and the next world. We cannot worry overmuch
about sickness, poverty, injustice, murder. Such things will
certainly always be around where there is man. Thus the
urgency of the problem can be submerged in the sands of
time.

Professor Sidney Hook, who certainly is one of America's
most delightful and incisive critics of religion and its incon-
sistencies—"the existence of God is logically compatible with
any political system whatsoever and with any feature within
it"—has scored the claims of religion to be truly effective in
fostering any real improvement in mankind.[10] "The representatives of [all] . . . religions . . . cannot agree concerning
which religion is the true one, and the only common belief
all religions seem to share is that all other religions are false,
a proposition which I find very persuasive."[11] The only possible conclusion Professor Hook can draw from this phenom-

enon is that God is not really responsible for anything significant in the realms of man:

> I speak from the standpoint of a naturalistic humanist for whom
> no traditional religion is adequate, and who cannot subscribe, on
> the basis of evidence and reason, to the proposition which Arnold
> Toynbee regards as the least common denominator of all re-
> ligions, viz.: "that man is not the spiritually highest presence
> known to man."[12]

What is meaningful for man is thus what man does. The
history of religion, of the Church, is one of tardy acceptance
of what man finally forges for himself. And while there may
be something shrewdly prudent and pragmatic in the openness to human worth we find on all sides, still ecclesiastical
and religious sources can claim little credit for it.

The silence of God presents a serious problem, therefore,
because it underscores the widespread suspicion that the
world is a "world without logos," to use Herbert Marcuse's
apt phrase; the fear that the very structure of physical and
human reality has no need of a place for God, that man is, in
truth, the highest spiritual presence known to man after all.[13]
If the voices of religion and the Churches seem venal and
insipid, as they often do to the world, is it not factually just
another proof that there is no voice of God in them, that
they stand on the periphery of mankind intoning a language
long since outmoded by advances in science and knowledge?
Religion, it would seem in this view, can only have the
vicarious satisfaction of parroting what man has discovered
for himself.

MAN'S ORDER

The basic question about God, therefore, must be stated in a very different way today. The silence of God is not just due to the babel arising from conflicting religious aims and doctrines which causes static in an otherwise clear channel so that we cannot receive his voice. On the contrary, we are asking about the source of transmission, as it were. Is the static really interfering with anything? And the reason we can ask this question is that we can produce and put on this channel practically everything that we formerly held to belong wholly to God's sphere of activity. We are told that life will be produced in a laboratory within a few years. We can understand, and even replace to a great extent, the powers of the physical and societal universe. By experimentation and analysis, we know now what the universe and man are and can be. Therefore we need no "hypothesis" of God as their cause, since our knowledge and technique make man their source, not God. God, at least the hypothesis of God, may have performed historically the function of serving as a hopeful solution to what was not yet understood, but this hypothesis is no longer required. The voice of God becomes increasingly inaudible, the more we hear our own word in the world. The modern industrial society is, in fact, beginning to become independent of its own need for the very raw materials it once needed so desperately.[14] Man has advanced in more and more cases to the point where he can produce a substitute for what he lacks out of his own ingenuity. He seems to be dependent on himself alone.

We can also examine the silence of God from another

aspect. The so-called destruction of teleology, the scientific persuasion that the order in the world is not the manifestation of mind and being, but of chance and balance, has left us unable to say that anything is "for" anything else, that things "do" fit together because they "should" fit together, because that is what they are "for."[15] The most crucial result of this theory for man is that he ceases to be the beneficiary of a benevolent creator and becomes the product of the slimmest chance. Nothing is really "for" him, he is not "for" anything else. Yet man finds this conclusion a strange one. How is it that scientific knowledge belongs to man at all? Why is it that technology finds its proper meaning as an effort, a truly global effort, even a cosmic effort, to release man? Moreover, when man begins to look at the use and the scope of this endeavor, he finds himself more and more with all men on the face of the planet. It becomes difficult to escape the conclusion that man and the universe are interrelated, one belongs to, is somehow "for," the other. Furthermore, in view of the acceleration of this process whereby man comes to cover the earth with his power, tools, and knowledge, few would any longer maintain that man is "for" the earth; rather, the opposite is true, the earth is "for" man. But this implies some order, indeed some given order.

Obviously, this order is not yet fully created, but only in the process of creation by man. Must this mean, therefore, that God is even more forcefully silenced? Is this man's world and work alone? It is at this point, at the point of the growing public recognition that the human race does have a specific global task, that we must stop for a moment in our inquiry about the silence of God. For the Christian especially, this is of great significance, since the Scriptures speak to mankind as to one man, to one person, as it were, who involves all men.[16] If we seriously examine the purpose of our technology, as well as the terrestrial and theoretic presuppositions which make it possible, we can see that its aim is precisely to free man from the "toil" aspect of his connection with nature. We see that the existence of elites in every society has been made possible by the toil of the many. Yet we also see that the evolution of modern society has not been in the direction of destroying elites—which have performed the task of safeguarding and expanding social development—but rather in the direction of passing on the social, material, and cultural riches of the elites to all men. This effort of distribution has been facilitated by the recognition and use of knowledge and techniques. Raymond Aron has sagely put his finger on the consequences in terms of social progress of a failure to accept what man has learned: "Nations which deliberately reject scientific development are choosing to leave the path of history and to stagnate in a backwater. Those which reject it unwittingly would appear doomed to final annihilation."[17]

Yet, apart from the question of "backward" nations, there is the further question of whether there is a tragic flaw in our society due to the superior condition of the elites in the world, especially the white elites. Undoubtedly there is some truth in the claim that this is the product of injustice rather than the product of a superior effort to develop and utilize knowledge and techniques, but it is by no means the whole truth. The fact is that this is a progress which necessarily takes time in order to spread to all nations.[18] The Belgian theologian M. Kuppens has stated the issue precisely:

The result of this is that the contacts with developed countries propagate in the souls of the less developed lands the contagion of our needs. The inequalities which actually exist are perceived in juxtaposition to the possibility which also exists of redressing them among all peoples. *These inequalities are seen as an injustice.* For that injustice, the whites are accounted responsible.[19]

The issue at stake here is between a commonly accepted goal and the speed and means with which it can be reached. The major hope of the world is to be given sufficient time and patience to expand and apply what we know and are coming to know. In truth, it does not seem to be primarily a question of justice and injustice, though that does enter into the problem of distribution and participation; rather it is the tragic slowness and difficulty involved in being a man with limits and imperfections, in belonging to a race which must act in time.

For this reason, a good part of the ferment in the world today is what we might call theological in origin—that is, arising from the confusion of the question of justice with that of human limitations. This is the problem of human finiteness to which we shall return in a later discussion; it involves man's recognition that he is not, in fact, God. The text of *The Church in the Modern World* has sensed something of this ferment:

Our contemporaries are coming to feel these inequalities with an ever sharper awareness. For they are thoroughly convinced that the wider technical and economic potential which the modern world enjoys can and should correct this unhappy state of affairs.[20]

Yet the thesis of exploitation is becoming more and more obviously out-of-date as an explanation for our modern difficulties in society. For the problem is not exploitation but rather membership in a creative industrial society:

The citizen of the rich world sees himself as fully earning the privileged position in which he sits. To the poor he has earned nothing. And we should be humble enough to remember that it is Western society which is productive, and not necessarily we as individuals. The economics of the matter are complex, but as a practical fact a cobbler or a college professor in Calcutta, working at his bench or addressing his class, can perform with exactly the same effort and skill as his opposite number in Chicago, and his real income is at the most favorable one-fifth as much. For a long while the citizen of Calcutta has thought this was so because in some invisible way the Chicagoan was exploiting him. With the advance of Western technology and the consequent increasing separateness of the rich and the poor on their opposite sides of the world the absurdity of the notion of exploitation will become more and more patent.[21]

The primary question, then, is not so much one of the unjust division of worldly goods as it is one of the creation of a society in whose progress and benefits all men can participate.

The Soviet physical chemist and Nobel prize winner Professor Nikolai Semenov has recently written a remarkable summary of what mankind can expect from "the world of the future." In the context of the silence of God and the mission of man, it is very worthwhile to pay some attention to Professor Semenov's observations. "On the basis of the rapid development of science and hence of technology," he writes, "the satisfaction, at a very high level, of all the material and spiritual needs of every man is a real possibility for the first time in history."[22] Professor Semenov then details the prospects for power development in the next decades, a development which he rightly argues to be the key to the humanization of this planet on the physical side for man. "As a result of full automation, working hours will be reduced to three or four hours a day. People will be able to devote all the rest of their time to sport, gardening, art, social activities, people's theaters, literature, and scientific and technical research. . . ."[23] Clearly, in this view, the technological development is "for" man as its goal. Furthermore, this ideal is not so much to reduce the elites to the level of the masses as to raise the masses to the level of the elites by the use of power and knowledge:

The ideal of social progress can be approximately formulated as the maximum happiness for the maximum number of people. The first precondition of this is full satisfaction of the material and cultural need of every man on earth. However, the satisfaction of material needs in itself is not enough for a happy life, though it is the chief and necessary precondition for the full spiritual activity of man. But by his nature man is not only a consumer but also a creator of material and spiritual values. The need of creative activity is not only one of the noblest but also one of the deepest, most ineradicable needs of man. Our greatest task is to bring varied creative activities within the reach of the broad mass of people. . . .

To demonstrate his creative ability and derive pleasure from doing so, every man must have a certain level of knowledge and development of his mind and feelings, of esthetic tastes, and a moral attitude to society and himself. This can be achieved if economic and social conditions are created to ensure the all-round development and creative labor of people.[24]

We have here, then, the final insight into the silence of God, since we have begun to reestablish a teleology in nature through science and technology, a teleology which is clearly man-oriented, a teleology within the confines of humanity, a teleology summed up by providing the greatest material, cultural, and spiritual welfare to all men. The degree to which the Soviet scientist grasps these basic trends in modern life is remarkable.

THE CENTRALITY OF MAN

But our topic is the silence of God. If we examine all the reasons alleged for God's silence, we cannot but be struck by the fact that the major reasons God is said to be silent are all, almost without exception, connected with the failure of ecclesiastical, religious man to be on the side of the true interests of man in the world. The suspicion widely exists that spiritual leaders by their silence or tacit cooperation too often seem to condone, or to hesitate before, evils or disorders that all men must condemn. The image of religion has not been positive in our times, leadership has not been found in its ranks. The reason given for this widespread opinion that the Church seems to be irrelevant or inimical to social justice and freedom is that the Church has not appeared to be in practice consistently on the side of man and his vocation in the world. "In the life of the People of God . . . there has at times appeared a way of acting that was hardly in accord with the spirit of the Gospel, or even opposed to it."[25] It is clear today that any man or any institution which fails to recognize the true dignity and potential of man will be cast aside.

In this struggle, we might well ask ourselves, Whose side is God on? In brief, we can say today with certainty and firmness that *God is always on the side of him who is on man's side.* This is the very meaning of the incarnational principle that God did become man to save, to redeem, what was in man. The reason God has appeared to be officially silent in these evolutions by which man has come to recognize his centrality and his mission has been primarily a theology of false dichotomy. This dichotomy can be stated in two propositions: (1) God cannot act where man acts, and (2) the purpose of God does not include the purpose of man. But we have now come to see more clearly that the free activity of man in forging his destiny on this earth, precisely because it is free and therefore properly man's, is also God's activity, since God wills man to be man. "According to the almost unanimous opinion of believers and unbelievers alike, all things on earth should be related to man as their center and crown."[26] And man, therefore, is a being with a dignity, a vocation—with something to do in this world. This "something to do" is precisely his relation to the physical world, and through it his relation to his fellow men. "If the fundamental precept of Christian love of one's neighbor," R. C. Kwant continues,

is to take concrete shape in a manner adjusted to the realities of the world in which we live, what will be required is an actual and deeply human concern for those realities. Such a concern has not infrequently been wanting, owing to a too exclusive solicitude for personal salvation, and a personal relation toward God. This reproach makes itself felt the more strongly in our days, when technical and social developments have created a framework of life in which it becomes increasingly clear that concern for one's own spiritual welfare cannot bear fruit except as part of a corporate responsibility for the entire human family.[27]

It is here that the silence of God comes to an end. For we discover the sense in which the humanist argument that man is the highest spiritual presence known to man is valid. It is this partial truth which makes the humanist so sure he is right. God has so loved the world that he has sent his only-begotten Son into it. Thus, whenever God is presented as opposed to man's freedom and his dignity, the atheist humanist, whether Marxist or secularist, rejects God, because he knows with certainty that man does belong to this world in some fundamental way.

This is a tragic rejection. For the dignity of man's task in the world and the freedom in which it is carried out imply not a God of silence, remote from his creatures, but one who has spoken to men. Our concept of God takes on an immensely greater depth of meaning when we become aware of his power to create a truly free creature with a task in the world. Once we recognize this—and we shall come back to this point—it becomes evident that God is present to man in the carrying out of his task. For this is the arena of God-given freedom in which man has power to decide whether he will accept his fellow man in love, and through him his God. This is what the First Epistle of John is about. We are back again to the scribes and the Pharisees, to Matthew and the Samaritan and the Magdalene. For the vocation man receives from God is not simply to achieve man's vocation as a human being, although it is at least this, but to achieve this vocation in a free service of love for his fellow men and there to participate in the life of God, which is the model and end of all our activities. Consequently, whenever we see movements which truly tend towards this design in that they are conformed to man's total vocation in the world, we can be sure that God is present in them, to the extent that the vision by which they are inspired is truly alive:

> The People of God believes that it is led by the Spirit of the Lord, who fills the earth. Motivated by this faith, it labors to decipher authentic signs of God's presence and purpose in the happenings, needs, and desires in which this People has a part along with other men of our age. For Faith throws a new light on everything, manifests God' design for man's total vocation, and thus directs the mind to solutions which are fully human.[28]

It is in this context that we discover the absoluteness of God's commitment to the creation he has brought forth.

THE PROJECT OF MAN

We are conscious, however, that the temporal vocation of man is a project for men to carry out. In this sense, it has a terminus. Nor must we forget that this project, since it is a product of freedom, can be achieved contrary to God's plan and therefore against man's interests. None the less, it seems true to say that God's causes are impeded most when his official or charismatic representatives appear to the world to be unworthy of their calling, to be opposed to man's earthly welfare and dignity. For this gives the cause of evil the one indispensable weapon it needs to attack God in the world—namely, a true but limited human good to promote. Such is the power of God that he is not ultimately defeated by any evil. This is the meaning of the Redemption. However, it is conceivable, indeed perhaps inevitable, that the whole temporal mission of man in the world should be presented to him in terms of that good most opposed to God's plan—that the choice given man should be between God and mammon. Needless to say, should this happen, it will be the tragic result of multiple failures of the children of light to be effectively on the side of man in the world; on the side, that is, of those with whom God has identified himself, the "little ones" of the Scriptures.

Nevertheless, man's mission in the world is a goal to be achieved freely, with the slowness and labor that is part of the finiteness of man. It is important to recognize this because it reminds us that the historical community of man in the world is made up of men with a human mission; men who will die. The significance of man is not a matter of when he is born—whether he will be born into those future generations who, profiting from the advances of technology and knowledge, will live in a more fully human condition on earth. What counts is whether he has worked for his fellow men, participated in the mission of serving others. This test of service is the one that ultimately determines his destiny. The human race returns to God through individual persons, each of whom achieves the purpose of God's creation, each of whom in eternity is to share in the life of the society which is the Trinity. But in this destiny, mankind is as one in Christ, the human race is divinized after the manner of the Son, of that person in the Trinity who eternally receives from the Father the divine life which he pours forth.

In the end, therefore, the whole gigantic historical effort of man to humanize creation in the service of his fellow man is vain and empty unless the destinies of the persons who contribute to this effort are each achieved in a common society before the Father. This is why the metaphysical and religious meaning of death—that is, of one's ultimate orientation with regard to the work which God is accomplishing in the world through man—is the final locus of God's voice and call. Christians, and through Christ all men, are destined for community. And community, even divine community, is of its very nature a community of the free, indeed a community of friends. And it would seem strange if the lesson man learned from his association with earth and with other men, the lesson of sharing and mission, of love and communication, should cease at the personal death of the members of the species.

The silence of God is broken, however, exactly here, for the word of God is in truth that of life, eternal life, for the race of man, for the man who, in loving his fellows, has come to realize that his life is somehow extended beyond death into the divine community, the community to which the race is called in the context of its earthly mission.

We discover in this theme of the silence of God, therefore,

that we cannot look for God anywhere apart from man and the mission given to him, for he is not to be found elsewhere. The depth and breadth of God's wisdom is seen only when we comprehend the significance which he has given to the physical universe and man's place in it. Hence we do not exalt God when we minimize the importance of man or of the creation but rather the opposite: we exalt God when we begin fully to appreciate the magnificence of creation and of man and the destiny of both. Yet if it is man's destiny to carry out a real task that God has given to him and to be with God, we must, so far as we can, learn more about creation and man, but especially about God—who he is, in what sense he is unique, what God's reality means to man. Thus the very silence of God leads us to the point at which God has broken his silence, to the Incarnation, to the revelation of the Father, the Son, and the Spirit.

NOTES

1. Cf. the incident of Thomas after the Resurrection, his demand for a sign. To Thomas' affirmation of faith the Lord replied: "You believe because you can see me. Happy are those who have not seen and yet believe." (John 20:29) Excerpts from *The Jerusalem Bible*, copyright © 1966 by Darton, Longman & Todd, Ltd. and Doubleday & Company, Inc. Reprinted by permission of the publishers.

2. R. C. Kwant, *Tijdschrift voor Theologie*, III, 3 (1963), p. 282.

3. John O'Connor, *America*, April 9, 1966, p. 484.

4. Jerome Kerwin, "Introduction" to E. A. Goerner, *Peter and*

Caesar (New York: Herder and Herder, 1965). For an excellent recent study of the anguish unenlightened ecclesiastical policy can cause, cf. Carmen Irizarry, *The Third Thousand* (New York: Harcourt, Brace, and World, 1966).

5. For a series of Council discussions on these topics, cf. *Council Speeches of Vatican II*, ed. by Hans Küng, Yves Congar, and Daniel O'Hanlon (Glen Rock, N.J.: Deus Books, 1964), pp. 79–144.

6. Cf. Charles N. R. McCoy, *The Structure of Political Thought* (New York: McGraw-Hill, 1963), chapter v.

7. "The present code [of Canon Law] takes no cognizance of Anglo-Saxon Common Law traditions, traditions recognized and accepted in practically every English-speaking country in the world. If the legal system of the Church were left not to Rome but to the episcopal conference in each nation, it is conceivable that here in America a balance could and would be restored between the legislative, judicial, and executive organs of power in the Church. At present the balance is seriously disturbed, the overwhelming weight of power is with the executive and administrative offices." Peter M. Shannon, "Changing Law in a Changing Church," *America*, February 18, 1967, p. 250.

8. Gerhard Szczesny, *The Future of Unbelief* (New York: George Braziller, 1961).

9. Archibald MacLeish, *An Epistle Buried in the Earth* (Boston: Houghton Mifflin).

10. Sidney Hook, "Law and Religion," Proceedings of Judicial Conference of the Tenth Judicial Circuit, *Federal Rules Decisions*, January 1964, p. 77.

11. *Ibid.*, p. 72.

12. *Ibid.*, p. 74.

13. Herbert Marcuse, "World without Logos," *Bulletin of the Atomic Scientists*.

14. Cf. Nathan Keyfitz, "Privilege and Poverty: Two Worlds on One Planet," *Bulletin of the Atomic Scientists*, March 1966, pp. 9–14.

15. Cf. Ernest Cassirer, *An Essay on Man* (Garden City, N.Y.: Doubleday Anchor, 1944), pp. 15–41.

16. Cf. Romans 5, 6.

17. Raymond Aron, *Bulletin of the Atomic Scientists,* January 1964, p. 23.

18. Cf. Keyfitz, *loc. cit.*

19. M. Kuppens, *Revue Ecclésiastique de Liége,* January 1964, p. 78.

20. "The Church Today," *The Documents of Vatican II,* ed. W. Abbott, p. 272. Excerpts from the Constitutions and Declarations of the Ecumenical Council are taken from *The Documents of Vatican II,* published by Guild Press, America Press, Association Press, and Herder and Herder, and copyrighted 1966 by The America Press. Used by permission.

21. Keyfitz, *loc. cit.*, p. 14.

22. "The World of the Future" by Nikolai Semenov is reprinted with permission from the February 1964 issue of the *Bulletin of the Atomic Scientists.* Copyright 1964 by the Educational Foundation for Nuclear Science.

23. *Ibid.*, p. 15.

24. *Ibid.*

25. "Declaration on Religious Freedom," *The Documents of Vatican II,* ed. W. Abbott, no. 12, p. 692.

26. "The Church Today," *The Documents of Vatican II,* ed. W. Abbott, no. 12, p. 210.

27. Kwant, *loc. cit.*, p. 282.

28. "The Church Today," *The Documents of Vatican II,* ed. W. Abbott, no. 11, p. 209.

3
The Trinity: God Is Not Alone

Questions about the meaning and destiny of man constantly arise in modern literature, as we have seen, and in modern societal thought; the hope for redemption and the longing to hear the voice of God in the world are realities of our times. But the modern world has had the greatest difficulty in understanding the reality of God which Christians feel is the answer to questions that all modern men are asking. It is, therefore, of some importance to present, in a manner as clear and as simple as possible, the meaning of the Christian God, to see why it is that precisely the Christian view of God can provide the key enabling us in some sense to unlock the mysteries of God as they are related to man in the world.

Christians agree with Moslems and Jews that God is one. "Yahweh, there is no one like you!" (Jeremiah 10:6) "Listen, Israel: Yahweh our God is the one Yahweh. You shall love Yahweh your God with all your heart, with all your soul, with all your strength." (Deuteronomy 6:4) This is the legacy that Christians have received from Israel. It is something they must believe in order to be Christians. Christians can, moreover, agree with the Greeks and the Romans that God transcends the cosmos, yet is everywhere present in the world. They can even agree, in some part, with those oriental traditions which exalt God by teaching man to abandon himself to the All, rejecting too much confidence in passing things. Christian tradition in the best sense has wisely sought to be universal in outlook, seeking to accept all that is true and valuable in the beliefs and values of other men.[1] To respect and accept the truth contained in other religions is not just a practical expedient, but a fundamental aspect of the Christian's openness to reality. The Christian must accept what is true wherever it may be found and from who ever may be discovered holding it. The unity of truth ultimately means at least this.

Yet, in reflecting on the long-term consequences of this willingness to accept the truth wherever found, we cannot ignore the fact that often in modern literature and thought it is the Christian who seems to inherit the task of defending what may be termed the "minimal" God, the God specifically shorn of all distinctions and unique characteristics, a kind of common entity in whom as many men as possible can believe without violence being done to anyone's intellectual assumptions. The Christian is thus expected to be the man who can "prove" that God exists, that he is all-powerful, all-knowing, the ruler of all.

When the Christian has completed this task, which is, in its positive sense, surely a vital part of his mission, he is often tempted to relax in the hope that now he has done what he can for the cause of God. But this approach (very laudable in itself) of searching for and accepting whatever element of God may be found anywhere among men has one very unfortunate drawback. In the Epistle to the Hebrews (11:6), a very useful and famous passage describes the minimal doctrines that a man must believe about God, namely, that he exists and that he rewards the good and punishes the evil. In discussing this minimum requirement, theologians add that, ideally speaking, the doctrines of the Trinity and the Incarnation should also normally be believed.[2]

Yet when we compare the content of the doctrines of the Trinity and the Incarnation with those minimal beliefs found in Hebrews, it becomes quite evident that the Trinity and the Incarnation describe something distinctively Christian, while the fact that God exists as a rewarder and punisher is a belief that can be shared by many non-Christians. In other words, the full Christian vision includes, indeed requires, the Trinity and the Incarnation in addition to whatever else might be accepted about God from reason or tradition. The Trinity and the Incarnation are *the* realities about God, about his internal life, about what he does in the world, about his relation to human society. The Trinity and the Incarnation are the realities that govern any Christian discussion of God and the world. In treating reality, Christianity finds its greatest richness in reflecting on these two unique aspects of its faith. Christianity gazes at the world through the eyes of these distinctive doctrines of the Trinity and the Incarnation.

There is, however, a certain paradox here of more than ordinary significance. The evolution within Christianity of its own willingness to accept and encourage the truths and developments found outside itself, of its ability to use pagan philosophers and to accept the spiritual insights and customs of other religions, its gradual openness to science and art, its growing sympathy with the faith of all men of good will, its conciliar effort to understand even the atheist—all these have made possible, almost for the first time, its own full comprehension of itself and of its belief in the Trinity and the Incarnation in the light of the vastness of the cosmos, of nature and man. Yet, as the early Creeds recall to our minds, everything distinctive in the Christian faith is included in these two doctrines of the Trinity and the Incarnation.[3]

With the recent thought of Christianity again focused upon its theoretic basis and upon its significance in the world, there is, therefore, some value in setting forth the long-range implications of these fundamental Christian beliefs as they are reflected in and projected upon the universe and man. We must see in what sense, for man also, the beginning is also the end; in what sense the meaning of the universe stems from and ends in the life of God, in eternal life. For the Christian, the richness and fecundity of the life of God is the explanation and the justification for the glorious, bewildering complexity discovered everywhere in history, in the cosmos, in life, in society, in man himself. Moreover, the life of God, eternal life, is properly man's destiny, his destiny as the total group of men—the city, as Augustine called it, of persons sharing this divine life. In some fashion, we must recognize the unity we have with other men in our common relation to God, in our common presence before him and before each other.

A PERFECT AND COMPLETE INNER LIFE

What men think of God permeates what they think of everything else. Historically, and even metaphysically, men have always encountered one primary embarrassment in thinking of God. God is believed to be one; as we have just seen, there are to be no gods like unto him. Even in polytheist concepts, there always seemed to be a place for a king-god, one unlike the rest. The idea that God is one seems almost of necessity to suggest the further, less easily acceptable, implication that God is also alone; that God, like man in modern literature, is also lonely. And no matter how man grapples with this conclusion that God is alone, no matter how rigidly inevitable it may seem, man finds, none the less, the aloneness of God quite unacceptable psychologically; indeed he finds the idea just a bit frightening. Even supposing that this one God is Love, with infinite tenderness towards all that is, still the very notion of God having no other, equal to himself, with whom to communicate is repellent. In this respect, God would seem to have been created, if it might be put in this way, just a little lower than man. Hence, we suspect, the primary reason for the many gods of polytheism is precisely this difficulty in believing in one, isolated, majestic God.

Nevertheless God is one God. The argumentation for this truth seems unassailable. Whatever the lines of reasoning we might take to arrive at the fact of God, all converge upon one God. The hypothesis of two Gods simply cannot be thought of as existing. Every man's native logic takes this for granted.

However, not all explanations of the one-God concept are

equally fortunate. Men are model-builders; they conceive
their worlds and their gods in some manner after their own
experience of life. It is right that they should do this, of
course, for their sensory experience does constitute their
primary avenue to reality. But we are in control of our
models; we can in a very real sense fashion them according
to what we choose to see. The almost inevitable effect of this
with respect to the one-God concept, however, if it is understood in terms of man's experience, is that the subject-ruler
relationship which he finds everywhere in the creation is applied to God, so that aloofness and dominance become for
him the natural images of God's reality. Such images can
strongly color our view of God without our realizing it, and
may even distort it. It might even be argued, therefore, that
the importance of the image we have of God can be judged
by the fact that God himself revealed how men were to conceive him: "Philip said, 'Lord, let us see the Father and then
we shall be satisfied.' 'Have I been with you all this time,
Philip,' said Jesus to him, 'and you still do not know me? To
have seen me is to have seen the Father. . . .'" (John 14:8–9)

In looking at the teaching of Christ in the New Testament,
we quickly discover that he did affirm that God is one, he did
accept the Hebrew notion of God. (Cf. Mark 12:29.) Yet
the Christian God is triune. The term "trinity" was, of course,
coined several hundred years after the death of Christ, probably by Tertullian. Neither Christ, nor the Apostles, nor Paul,
nor the Evangelists used it. Christian theology and tradition
have come to use it to define the sense, revealed in the New
Testament, in which God is triune. In the Gospels and

Epistles there is, strictly speaking, no formal treatment of the internal life of God as such. Everything that we know about the vast riches of God's proper life comes through the New Testament, to be sure, but it comes indirectly from examining and explaining what is related in Scripture concerning the Son of God's incarnate life and mission. The Father, the Son, and the Spirit are manifested as participants in the process of redemption. Furthermore, the more profound passages about the life of God, those of John and Paul, are usually the reflections of these writers, more penetrating illuminations about the simple phrases of the baptismal formulas or the utterances of the Lord. We might almost maintain with some justice that the central teaching of Christianity about God, namely, that regarding God's trinitarian life, was not Christ's first concern. Yet, even though we accept that the New Testament teaches primarily about the way to salvation rather than about the inner life of God, which in its fullness we can only begin to know in the Beatific Vision, we still feel our need to understand something about the latter. We are aware that the New Testament speaks of the Holy Spirit as a person: he is sent, he sanctifies, he teaches. We are taught that all men are redeemed in Christ by the Father through the Spirit, but we are not really satisfied intellectually by what we can learn in Scripture about the Spirit's exact significance.

All this is but another way of saying that the inner life of God is a mystery, which cannot be fully open and comprehensible to men. It is something only God himself can comprehend fully: "After all, the depths of a man can only be known by his own spirit, not by any other man, and in the same way the depths of God can only be known by the Spirit of God." (1 Corinthians 2:11)

Nevertheless, though the mystery will remain, we can learn from the New Testament that this life of God is one of a community of love between three persons. They are distinct: the Son is not the Father but receives the divine nature from him; the Holy Spirit is not the Son but receives the divine nature in the love poured forth from the Father and the Son. Each is constituted a person by his relation to the others in the godhead. Each fully possesses the divine nature, sharing a community of life in one divine reality.

That God is triune is, therefore, the great Christian truth about God in himself. Later on we shall explore more fully this sketch of the doctrine. Here we wish to stress only this aspect of its meaning: that in the godhead there is "diversity," since each person is "another." "This is the statement about the Holy Trinity: it ought to be spoken of and believed not as triple but as Trinity. Nor can it be rightly said that in one God is Trinity, but rather that one God is Trinity."[4] The revelation of the Trinity, even in this imperfect manner, is the ultimate truth of the Christian faith. The Trinity confirms our feeling that it is not good for God to be alone; our instincts are right about the inadequacy of a solitary God.[5] God is unity and community. The Christian vision, therefore, must begin with the Trinity. For if we fail to grasp this truth about God, all else will be of little real value when it comes to understanding the nature and destiny of the world and of ourselves.

It is customary in theology to make a division between those truths about God which can be derived from nature by reason and those derived from revelation. Truth itself demands that such a distinction be maintained; it is important to establish the category to which the knowledge in question belongs. However, to whatever category a specific truth belongs, when we are dealing with the inner life of the living God it is imperative that we see it within the whole structure of reality— that we should recall what God is, what man is, and what the world is.

God did not first create man and then, after some lapse of time, "elevate" him to a higher state. On the contrary, he created the universe for man called from the beginning to live the divine life as a gift. This does not make God's action in giving man a share in his trinitarian life any less gratuitous; what it does indicate is that the whole of human life along with the cosmic reality which is ordained to it will be reflective primarily of the trinitarian life of God. Hence if man and nature are to be understood in their Christian fullness, we must meditate with all the powers of our mind on the trinitarian life which is the source and model of all reality. This need to relate the life of the Trinity to the rest of reality is one of the great challenges of modern thought. It will not mean trying to "deduce" human and cosmic foundations from the life of God; rather, it will mean an effort to see the implications of the fact that God's inner life is both that which reality itself reflects and that to which man, and through him the cosmos, is destined. So revolutionary is the import of the revelation of the Trinity that a vision of reality in its light is required. For this truth transforms all others in a most startling and transcendent manner.

THE LIFE OF GOD AND CREATION

God is Trinity. If we accept the idea of God as creator, we can logically assume that whatever begins and ends in him will somehow be like him. The creation itself does not, of course, reveal the difference of persons in God. The fact that God is triune and the highest creatures have a special relation to the trinitarian life is something we know by revelation.

Scripture and theological reflection have provided some precious insights into the inner life of God. Perhaps the very first notion that comes to mind is the fact itself that it is a *life*, a complete life. One of the classical difficulties with the one-God or monistic concept (and a perennial source of doctrinal deviation in Christian history) has been the conjecture that God must somehow need the world because he would be incomplete without it. This notion has often been grounded in a seemingly legitimate and laudable effort to exalt the dignity of man and creation. The idea was that God was incomplete without man and creation, so that through his need of them they necessarily participated in the dignity of the divinity. The ironic aspect of this is that the universe and man are really more exalted if God does *not* need them. The problem is, Why does not God need them? And the ultimate answer is the trinitarian life.

We can progress somewhat more deeply into this problem by reflecting on the notion of worship. Contemplation carries with it the idea of receptivity, of being given what is not possessed. Worship is based on contemplation, but the concepts of rejoicing and praise are added when it is applied to the contemplation of God. So worship is the act of man rejoicing in the simple fact of God—Let God be God! to use Luther's wonderful phrase. God is transcendent, he is what he is, who he is. God, in other words, is not subject to change. He is complete life in himself, he requires no intrinsic assistance outside himself. God is absolute, complete, and total in himself. When man worships God, he means precisely to accept this truth, that the reality of God, his life and activity, are in and for God himself. The relation between God and all else is such that God *requires* nothing but his own life. This completeness of God does not minimize the realities outside God. Quite the contrary, it indicates the primary truth about God—namely, that his trinitarian life really is complete in itself, and this truth, as we shall presently see, is the essential and magnificent foundation of the dignity of creatures.

From the New Testament we know that God so loved the world that he sent his only-begotten Son. (1 John 4:9). God is concerned with the world. At first sight this seems to be an enormously consoling doctrine. But is it? To maintain that God is concerned with the world is by no means reassuring if that concern is a deterministic thing in God. In such a case, any degree of warmth or support that could flow out of God's concern would vanish, since it would merely be a function of an organized system. Right at this point, the issue of the trinitarian God arises in its most meaningful form. A God with no diversity of persons, a monolithic God, must seemingly look outside himself to the world as the primary arena of his activity. And by hypothesis, this relationship to the world must necessarily be one of inequality such that the relation is primarily, as we have already suggested in another context, one of mastery and dominance. This superiority could express itself as a fate in which all events are in fact predetermined or as a caprice in which all set order is capable of being set at naught. In any case, since the life of a monolithic God would be difficult to explain by and of itself, it would apparently have to find its primary meaning in relationship with the world. The Trinity, of course, cannot be "demonstrated" from reason. It is possible to conceive of God as infinitely one, with infinite power, knowledge, love, and wisdom. Yet, such a God is aloof, and almost by default we are led to presume that the essential activity of such a God is concern for the world since both knowledge and love seem to imply otherness, even otherness of persons.[6]

Such a consequence, then, brings us back to the Trinity. The doctrine says that the godhead is manifested in and completed by three distinct persons who equally possess, but in different ways, one divine life. God is not some fourth essence apart from the three; three persons are one God.[7] In other words, the three persons have an inexhaustible love and life in themselves. Let us note what follows from this. Since the Trinity have a complete life within the godhead, all that is outside their life is related to these persons *not* by necessity but by love and choice. The world thus exists because of the independence and freedom of God. This is made possible by the prior fullness and completeness of the trinitarian life.[8] We can take many attitudes towards the world in which we dwell. What we must now recognize is that, at bottom, it is a *chosen* universe, it is the product of a supreme, transcendent freedom, not coerced by any internal deficiency or exigence within God himself. As a result of the completeness of the internal life of God, everything else in the universe is the consequence of a free choice. Wherever we look, we ultimately see freedom, not necessity. And the contingent necessity we do see is thus rooted in the more basic freedom that brought reality outside God to be in the first place.

THE FATHER, THE SON, AND THE SPIRIT

From the ideas of life, worship, and the freedom of creation, the reality of God's own life manifests itself as something whole and complete in itself. But why is it whole and complete in itself? In God, three persons exist. As we have already said, each of these three persons is distinct, one is definitely not the other, each is different because of his relationship to the others. Theology describes this aspect of trinitarian life by affirming, as we have noted, that the persons in God are "relations."[9] This means that person in God is wholly unique and irreducible. One person is what he is, he cannot be the other; yet his total reality is "towards" the other. Person, in its every essence, then, is "other-oriented." There is and can be no person who is simply for and by himself alone. A person, in order to be a person, therefore, must be totally himself, yet wholly oriented towards, open to, other persons.

The inner life of God contains diversity and community within itself, both of which imply order. And in the relations that are persons in God, there is a definite, irreversible order of Father, Son, and Spirit.[10] The Father from all eternity begets the Son, from the Father and the Son proceeds the Spirit.[11] In the Holy Spirit, the internal life of God finds its completion in a person who *receives* all that he is from the others, but who is still a person who is God. This means that order and reception are not in their very essence opposed to freedom and diversity, since all three persons are God who is one.

Historically, Augustine in his book *De Trinitate* was the thinker who suggested that a diversity of life in God could be best understood after the model of intellection and volition. In his masterful analysis, Augustine suggested how it might be possible for there to be three persons, yet one God with one intellect and one will. Intellection and volition, he pointed out, are aspects of the human life of man. They are not outside him. Yet, by them the otherness and diversity of reality become man's to know, and through knowledge become man's to rejoice in, to go out to. These faculties clearly make man something more than a static being concerned only with himself. They imply that man's destiny is to be open to the knowledge and love of all things.

In the prologue to the Gospel of John it is said that the Word, whose glory was as that of the only-begotten of the Father, was made flesh. Generally in the New Testament, the Incarnation is conceived in terms of fatherhood and sonship. Since the essence of fatherhood is to beget a son to whom the father gives his own nature, and the essence of the generation of a word—or a thought—is the perfect expression of the mind which conceives it, we can see how the concepts of the second person as Son and as Word combine. In God is realized perfectly the desire to give to another all that one has, to have another as the perfect object of one's love.[12] The Son has received perfectly what the Father can give of himself. But the Father remains the Father and the Son remains the Son. The

Son is the godhead as originating from the Father who has no source, who from eternity is. This is part of the intimate life of the one God. The Son possesses the same nature as the Father, but he possesses this divine nature as received from someone, from the Father.

The Son loves the Father as the Father loves the Son. The gift of their love is what both share and wish to return. The Father, therefore, is pure origin, the Son both receives and gives. The Son receives the divine nature from the Father; together with the Father he gives it to the Spirit. The Spirit is pure reception within the godhead. Yet the Spirit is the starting point, as it were, of what is outside God. This is why all creation is essentially rooted in choice, gift and love, why it is rooted in the Spirit. (Cf. Wisdom, chapters 7, 8.)

Within the godhead, the Spirit completes the life of God. He provides the final element of diversity in God's inner life, he is God as pure gift. What the love between the Father and the Son yields is the Spirit. In human terms the value of a gift lies not so much in what it is as in what it represents. What any gift is in its essence—what we intend to give in it— is precisely ourselves. This does not mean that we shall cease in any sense to be ourselves or in any way deny the creative power of the other. On the contrary, both the giver and the one who receives rejoice in the acceptance implied of what each is. There is a perfection in the reality we are, an acceptance in it which suggests the final excellence of any communication, namely, the return of what we are in the hope that this is the greatest of all gifts. In the Trinity, there is in some higher sense the perfection of this human analogy. The Spirit is precisely God as gift, God as total acceptance, the perfect reception of the divine nature as received personally from the Father and the Son.

The Father as unbegotten origin of the divine life, therefore; the Son as the reflection, as the perfect Word and Son of the Father; the Spirit as gift, the perfect reception of the divine life from the Father and the Son all indicate that the divine life of persons, the one godhead, possesses an otherness and a vitality within it that fully contains itself. Personal being in God is totally related; even to be personality, all reality must reflect this openness to other persons. And since personal life in God is total giving and total receiving, the life of God is *societal*. And since this giving and receiving is mutual, complete and between persons, the life of God is fundamentally a friendship. The Trinity is friendship. All human life proceeding from the life of the Trinity, then, originates and ends in friendship. In other words, the fact that there is otherness in God, that persons are related to one another in God, means that the perfection of personal life, its metaphysical as well as its theological perfection, is friendship.

The Trinity, again, is friendship. And friendship requires that its members remain distinct. It is absolutely necessary that friends remain themselves while giving or receiving the new life of the friend whom they choose to love. Failure to perceive this exactly defines the great theoretical problem in Plato's *Symposium* in which love ends up by destroying the other.[13] Put in trinitarian terms, the Father is the Father, but begets the Son. The Son is the Son, but is the word of the Father. The Spirit is the Spirit, but he is the gift of the Father and the Son together. God is only God in otherness, in a distinction of persons. For Christians, the God who does not possess otherness within himself is not their God, since God is love, and love requires equality in diversity, order in unity. And it is this that has been revealed in the Father, the Son and the Spirit.

Is God free? Is it possible, for example, for there to be such a radical freedom in God that the Father might choose to be the Son instead, or the Son the Spirit? Might it even be that God could choose not to be God? Notions of freedom such as these questions imply presuppose that the freedom of the highest reality cannot be stable. God, the argument goes, should be free to be a rock, or a fish, or the whole universe. Of course, it seems quite obvious from the outset that if God should really choose to become a stone, for example, and should on this supposition proceed really to become one, he would cease to be God.

Freedom in God, then, and consequently in all being, cannot suggest the possibility of annihilation. God is, the persons are. Freedom finally refers either to a goal or reality not as yet achieved outside oneself or to the firmness and persistence of a choice already made. The choice to be something else, some other real being, is equivalent to self-annihilation, which is impossible.

Knowledge, of course, is, in one sense, the choice to be something else; love is the choice to share the life of someone else. But neither of these admits the possibility of annihilation; rather precisely the opposite, the stability and growth of the reality that is known and loved. Knowledge and love are the paths by which we become what we are not, by which we share what is outside us without destroying it. The freedom of God, therefore, refers to his possibility of creating outside himself and of loving what he has created, but this creation outside himself cannot mean creating another God.[14] God simply is not free to create another God. But he is free to create other beings who can share his life. The volition in God himself is the perfection, the absolute rest in the goodness and completeness of God's being itself. The importance of this is that God is ultimately God. This means that there is the possibility of an ultimate choice, of a final, permanent love that need not always be seeking for something else. In the end, because God is love, to love is to keep.

The divine life is one; this life is possessed by three persons each in his own way. The relationship of these persons to each other is not temporal—the Father is not older than the Son—though it is spoken of in this way out of the exigencies of our human conceptual framework. Rather, as we have seen, it is a question of different ways of possessing the same divine life. These three persons so complete in themselves the potentiality of divine life that there can be no other persons in God.[15] Since each of these persons truly differs from the other, since each acts as a person within the godhead, and since all else but each other they possess in common in the divine life, the whole reality of what it is to be a person is openness to and reception of another person. The life of God is of its very nature one life, but it is one life which is also a *koinwnia*, a communion, a fellowship, a society at its very heart. God is not alone.[16] The ultimate perfection of person, therefore, is not independence and isolation, but rather society, openness and commitment to others, communion with others in a common life and task.

Furthermore, since persons as such are permanently themselves, always radically retaining their distinction from others as independent lives, irreversible and unique—the Father does not become the Son, the Son does not become the Spirit —the diversity of persons is an integral part of personal communion.[17] Hence, any theory which involves the possibility of the merging of the person—be it the human person into God or the persons of God into each other—must be rejected. It follows from this that a society tends to diversity as well as to unity. The trinitarian foundation of this principle is the three persons in one nature. The model of the perfect society, therefore, is not a monism, a being without distinction.

The trinitarian life of God, then, reveals to us an unexpected richness. It is our hope, in this book, to explore some of its implications for modern society.

THE PROBLEM OF THE MAN-GOD

Previously, we mentioned that the New Testament is not primarily concerned with expounding the inner life of the Trinity, but with the Trinity as a factor in the Incarnation. The Incarnation is a means to the salvation of man which offers to man the ultimate possibility of sharing in the life of the Trinity. Now in the light of what we have seen of the trinitarian life, just what is the Incarnation and how does it relate to the Trinity? To introduce this subject, we can, perhaps, do no better than to recall the words of the devil in his discussion with Ivan Karamazov just before the trial of his brother Dmitri for the murder of their father. "As soon as men have all of them denied God," the devil muses to Ivan,

> . . . the old conception of the universe will fall of itself . . . and what's more the old morality, and everything will begin anew. Men will unite to take from life all it can give, but only for joy and happiness in the present world. Man will be lifted up with a spirit of divine Titanic pride and the man-god will appear. From hour to hour extending his conquest of nature infinitely by his will and science, man will feel such lofty joy from hour to hour in doing it that it will make up for all his old dreams of the joys of heaven. Everyone will know that he is mortal and will accept death proudly and serenely like a god. His pride will teach him that it's useless for him to repine at life's being a moment, and he will love his brother without need of reward. Love will be sufficient only for a moment of life, but the very consciousness of its momentariness will intensify its fire, which is now dissipated in dreams of eternal love beyond the grave.[18]

This passage which we have quoted at such length is important for many reasons, but primarily for the way in which it points up the problem of the Man-God and who he is. Dostoyevsky's devil has here described the alternative to God in classic terms. We would be imperceptive if we did not recognize in this passage much that is relevant to the belief of many of our contemporaries. Indeed we can even see our own temptations here. This vision of man as essentially and primarily dedicated to the transformation of this earthly life belongs, it seems well to note, to Christianity. Since this mis-

sion of world transformation is a true task of man, this charm-
ing devil of Dostoyevsky's can isolate it and pretend that it
is man's whole vocation. It is, of course, the sole practical
alternative to the trinitarian life as man's ultimate destiny.
God does indeed command the transformation of the world
by knowledge and science and service, but this effort is not to
be conceived as something divorced from the next life and
alien to it—a frequent temptation for Christians. The Christian vision of the world is precisely that in which the reality
of the world and its tasks comes to share through man in the
life of the Trinity.

In the light of the Incarnation and the Trinity, then, the
first thing we must recognize is that the very existence of the
Trinity—the fact of an everlasting life independent of creation, and consequently of ourselves—must always undermine
and render impermanent any satisfaction or content man may
have with the things which are merely of this world. Man
has two very real and powerful hopes, so basic that they constitute what he is. One is for the transformation and humanization of the earth on which he lives; the other is for everlasting
life, the life which is identified with the life of the Trinity.
For it is to share this life with other creatures that God has
created us in the first place. In Christianity these two goals, as
it were, the sharing in eternal life and the humanization of
creation, are one vision. Historically, man's humanity has
often enough been truncated by an overstress of the next life,
to the exclusion or minimization of the significance of his
human or earthly mission. Today, however, the opposite
temptation seems to be becoming more prevalent—that is, the

temptation to follow the suggestion of Ivan's devil to forget
God in pursuit of man in this world. The important thing
to note here is not that one or the other of these poles has
been too much stressed at one time or another, but that
both are essential to man. To be man is to neglect neither.

THE HUMANITY OF GOD

The problem remains. How is this possible? How can
eternal life be combined with the fleeting historical existence
of man in the world? The first truth of Christianity is that
God is triune. The second is that one of this Trinity, the Son,
became man.[19] Who is God? God is the Trinity. But this
must seem abstract and vague even after we have seen some
of the importance of this revelation. Our thoughts about God
will always tend to be nebulous until we clearly realize that
the second person became man. He took on the conditions
of finiteness in his very person. The second person, in assuming human nature in addition to his divine nature, by this
very act bridged the gulf between the inner life of the Trinity
and the life of man on earth. God has appeared among men.
In his birth, living, dying, rising again, and ascension, Jesus
Christ, that person of the Trinity who, without setting aside
his divinity, took on our humanity, is *forever* in the form of
God-man. As the Epistle to the Hebrews so beautifully puts
it:

Since in Jesus, the Son of God, we have the supreme high
priest who has gone through to the highest heaven, we must
never let go of the faith that we have professed. For it is not as if

we had a high priest who was incapable of feeling our weaknesses with us; but we have one who has been tempted in every way that we are, though he is without sin. . . . Then there used to be a great number of those other priests, because death put an end to each one of them; but this one, because he remains *for ever*, can never lose his priesthood. It follows, then, that his power to save is utterly certain, since he is living for ever to intercede for all who come to God through him. (Hebrews 4:14–15; 7:23–25)

Where Christ is, there is also the Father and the Spirit.

What does it mean that Christ became man? We have seen that the life of the Trinity is complete in itself. It has no need of anything beyond itself; it is itself the end, the perfect life. We have seen also that as a result of this perfect life, everything else in the universe is the product of divine freedom. We noted, further, that the very nature of person is such that it can be associated with others in society; that the essence of person, its very structure, is to be open to, related to, the other. Now if there is to be an expansion, as it were, of the life of the Trinity whereby other persons (finite ones necessarily, as there cannot be two Gods) share in its inner life, the only meaningful way this could happen would be if these finite persons freely chose such a life with the Trinity. The whole of the material and spiritual creation outside God—a creation modeled on the Son, as the prologue to John's Gospel tells us, in that person in the Trinity whose reality is the divine life as received and as giving—exists to make such a choice possible for men, to the end that their choice should be truly free, without the necessity that would arise if man were directly placed before the vision of God.

ETERNAL SALVATION IN THE FINITE,
HUMAN ORDER

The first choice that man had of accepting life with God was rejected by him. This rejection, however we conceive it, we call original sin.[20] We often hear complaints about this doctrine, admittedly not an easy one to comprehend. How is it just, it is asked, that we should be affected by an ancient ancestor? Yet, original sin is the dogma of the physical connection of all men to one another in their origin and destiny.[21] However original sin is conceived, it is the doctrine that men are bound together in some sin or alienation that only God can ultimately overcome. In a sense we can perhaps understand this doctrine somewhat better if we realize that men do have the chance, and indeed duty, of influencing others. The parents cannot ask their child if he wants to be born; the child cannot oppose the beginning of their profound influence over him, for better or for worse. All men are what they are in large part because of the choices of their immediate and remote forebears. Original sin suggests that this situation was true for the whole human race. In this sense it is the direct result of a true freedom given to finite, material persons to influence for good or ill all human life that originates within mankind.

Nevertheless original sin and the transmission of it did not deflect God's purpose in regard to man. Man's original choice was, to be sure, a rejection. But the finite will in this life is not something that need remain fixed. It can choose again, since it exists in time, in a constant condition of growth. For this reason, another means was initiated which sought to achieve God's original purpose of associating other persons with himself in the life of the Trinity:

> By an utterly free and mysterious decree of His own wisdom and goodness, the eternal Father created the whole world. His plan was to dignify men with a participation in His own divine life. He did not abandon men after they had fallen in Adam, but ceaselessly offered them helps to salvation, in anticipation of Christ the Redeemer, "who is the image of the invisible God, the firstborn of every creature" (Col. 1:15). All the elect, before time began, the Father "foreknew and predestined to become conformed to the image of his Son, that he should be the firstborn among many brethren" (Rom. 8:29).[22]

This new plan of God, then, is the cycle of the history of salvation leading from the promise to Adam, to Abraham, to Moses, to David, to the Jewish people, to Christ, and the passing on of this mission through the Apostles to all nations.[23] With the coming of Christ, true man and true God, with his life, death, and resurrection, the possibility of again choosing to live with God was offered to men. Salvation was to be achieved in associating mankind with Christ, our brother, to follow the path through death which Christ himself followed.

Christ, in accepting all the consequences of sin, transformed and redeemed all the suffering, all the finitude, and all the limitations of man in this passing world. Even death, the last barrier, was breached. "Death, where is your victory?" as Paul asked. (I Corinthians 15:55) In Christ's life, in the fact of the incredible event of the Incarnation, that event whereby the finiteness and infiniteness of reality merged into one another, all things proper to man as we know him were re-created in the blessing of the Lord's presence. And although sin, the last alienation from God, remains what it is, a free choice of man, still in Christ this choice too is forgiven and redeemed. "He looked up and said, 'Woman, where are they? Has no one condemned you?' 'No one, sir,' she replied. 'Neither do I condemn you,' said Jesus, 'go away, and don't sin any more.' " (John 8:10–11)

No choice against God can remain permanent for the man who is free to choose again in the grace brought by Christ. The act of sin reveals how truly we are bound up with all things, how all things are interconnected, and how all is related to God. Sin is, then, a very powerful negative witness to the importance of things. But sin is a choice that is always of something finite as if it were in isolation from all else. Thus sin is always for itself; indeed, for the self and against God, as God is found present in all the things he has created. Because Christ as God and man is himself concretely connected with all reality, the image of all creation, the firstborn among men, the damage of sin as it happens in the world can be repaired and transformed in him.

The destiny of mankind is to be saved by the Father through the Son in the Spirit. Mankind is to become Christ's brother; that is, it is to share the life of the Trinity, eternal life, as the Son shares it.

Something which has existed since the beginning, that we have heard, and we have seen with our own eyes; that we have

watched and touched with our hands: the Word, who is life—
this is our subject. That life was made visible: we saw it and we
are giving our testimony, telling you of the eternal life which
was with the Father and has been made visible to us. What we
have seen and heard we are telling you so that you too may be
in union with us, as we are in union with the Father and with
his Son Jesus Christ. (1 John 1:1–3)

But, as we have seen, the life of the Son in the Trinity is a
life that both gives and receives.[24] Man, therefore, to be truly
like the Son, must receive the divine life, which he does in the
gifts of creation and grace, but he must pass this life on to
others in the Spirit. This is man's mission in the world, his
mission of meaningfulness and choice wherein he actually
decides in the concrete historical order of his temporal life
whether he elects an eternal life with the Trinity in an openness of love and community. Here theology meets the hints
and the agonies of man as we have seen him in modern literature and society. The Christian dispensation is such that this
choice of eternal life with the persons of the Trinity is de-
cided by man's openness to his brother in the tasks of this
world, but to his brother who is so loved by Christ as to be
identified with him. "In so far as you did this to one of the
least of these brothers of mine, you did it to me." (Matthew
25:40) "Saul, Saul, why are you persecuting me?" (Acts
9:4)

From these observations on Christ and the Trinity we can
see that the Incarnation is God's effort, as it were, to conform
to human nature and to assume human destiny, with all ma-

terial creation and all human history, into the trinitarian life. And yet this action is so supremely conformed to man's dignity that it is ultimately an invitation, not a demand, not a coercion. The life of the Trinity is a personal life of love and freedom. No one can participate in it on any other terms. And this invitation does not come to man from some place in outer space or from somewhere in the obscure depths of the inner self; rather it comes through the new commandment that we shall love one another as Christ has loved us, that we shall live our lives in this gift of mutual openness and friendship. If we reflect deeply on the significance this has for Christian theology, we cannot help being moved by the truth that it means a constant transformation of the earth by the fullest use of our minds, hearts, and hands for the complete human fulfillment of the brothers in whom Christ is incarnated as his body, as Paul tells us. (Colossians 1:22)

THE SURPRISE OF GOD

We have, then, in Christianity, in its doctrines of the Trinity and the Incarnation, a simultaneous acceptance of the world—its demands, sorrows, and hopes—and eternal life, an eternal life of persons in society, in community, which through Christ unites mankind to the godhead. We should ponder the meaning and relevance of these basic Christian truths. The kind of God we believe in tells us what we are. We have seen how we must look on the world as something chosen by God in freedom and love; how creation is the basis for man's ability to make a free choice of God; how God in himself is a trinity of persons; how society and openness to other persons lie at the very heart of both ourselves and God; how the union we seek always retains the reality which we are.

What category or mode of thought is best to sum up what we as Christians are and have as a result of our common faith? What is the outlook on life and the world that best describes our faith? Somehow, the most precise description of this seems simply to be one of utter, complete surprise. This experience of surprise is one we should advert to more often in any case, but what is of importance here is that we will never be able fully to grasp that the Trinity and the Incarnation are really true until we can fully open ourselves to their abiding freshness and wonder, to the astounding and mysterious relationship they have to what we are in our own lives. Indeed, our capacity for being surprised by these things is part of our capacity for being surprised at all that surrounds us everywhere, both in the world of things and in the world of persons. We shall see in the next chapter something of the meaning of this sense of surprise for Christians as they face the physical world. In any case, when we have sensed some of the incredible wonder that things like ourselves should exist at all, when we have again seen the miracle, as it were, that the world itself is, we can better understand that it is the reawakening of this sense of surprise that will lead us most surely to that state of mind and heart whereby we can again look upon the Trinity and the Incarnation as the astonishing truths they are. For they are the truths of the inner life of God, of that foundation of all society that is the Trinity, of the total material and historical life of man with God in Christ.

NOTES

1. The Council documents on Ecumenism, Non-Christians, the Missions, and the Church in the Modern World are especially pertinent to this point.

2. The tradition of the Church on this point can be found in Denzinger, nos. 75, 2164, and 2380.

3. These creeds can be found in Denzinger, nos. 2–150.

4. This formula is found in the Eleventh Council of Toledo; Denzinger, no. 528.

5. "We believe in one God the Father Almighty and in one Lord Jesus Christ the Son of God and in one God the Holy Spirit. We worship and confess not three Gods, but Father, Son, and Holy Spirit as one God. Thus there is not one God who is, as it were, solitary; nor is the very one who is the Father also himself the Son, but the Father it is who begets, and the Son who is begotten, and the Spirit is not begotten or unbegotten, neither created nor made, but proceeding from the Father and the Son, coeternal, coequal, and cooperator with the Father and the Son. . . ." From the Formula "Fides Damasi" (about fifth century); Denzinger, no. 71. For fuller discussions of the doctrine see Denzinger, nos. 167, 367, 415, 441, 501, 525, 531, 542, 545, 616, 619, 2669.

6. Cf. Thomas Aquinas, *Summa Theologica*, I, 32, c. and ad 2.

7. ". . . Thus in God there is only a 'trinitas,' not a 'quaternitas'. . ." This expression is found in the Fourth Lateran Council, Denzinger, no. 804.

8. Cf. John H. Wright, *The Order of the Universe according to St. Thomas* (Rome: Gregorian University Press, 1957).

9. Cf. Denzinger, nos. 528, 532, 570, 800.

10. Cf. Denzinger, nos. 573, 805.

11. Cf. Denzinger, nos. 2–150, 800, 803.

12. Cf. August Brunner, "Vater und Sohn," *Geist und Leben*, 32 (1959), pp. 26–33.

13. Cf. Plato, *The Symposium*, tr. W. Hamilton, Penguin Classics.

14. Cf. Thomas Aquinas, *Summa Theologica*, I, 19–24.

15. Cf. Denzinger, no. 804.

16. "We believe and confess the most holy and omnipotent Trinity, Father, Son, and Holy Spirit, one God only but not solitary. . . ." Sixth Council of Toledo, Denzinger, no. 490.

17. "Nor do we say that just as there are three persons, so there are three substances, but rather one substance and three persons. For what is the Father is not ad se, but relative to the Son; and what is the Son is not ad se, but relative to the Father; likewise the Holy Spirit is not ad se, but is referred relatively to the Father and the Son in that the Spirit is predicated of the Father and of the Son. . . ." Eleventh Council of Toledo, Denzinger, no. 528.

18. Dostoyevsky, *op. cit.*, p. 628.

19. "We believe in his Son, our Lord Jesus Christ. . . ." St. Augustine, Denzinger, no. 21.

20. Cf. Denzinger, no. 1512.

21. The encyclical *Humani Generis* of Pius XII held that in the present state of our knowledge, the transmission of this sin seems to demand one pair of first parents. The problem of how this is to be interpreted is much discussed today. In general, however, it would seem that any theory of original sin, no matter how it is thought to be transmitted, will involve and connect the whole human race. Cf. Pierre Smulders, "Evolution and Original Sin," *Theology Digest*, Autumn 1965, pp. 172–176. Cf. Denzinger, nos. 3895–3898.

22. "Dogmatic Constitution on the Church," *The Documents of Vatican II*, ed. Walter Abbott, no. 2, p. 15.

23. Cf. "Dogmatic Constitution on Divine Revelation," in *ibid.*, pp. 111–128.

24. Cf. Denzinger, no. 800.

4

The Cosmos and Christianity: The World Is for Man

Our understanding of God, then, is important for our view of society. But the relation of the world to man and to God is also of prime importance. What is not God is, quite literally, not God. There cannot be two Gods, so that what is in fact not God will always manifest all the signs of "non-godness" —that is, there must be imperfection in the world. Only God is absolutely perfect. Yet the very fact that God is God means that whatever exists outside God, with whatever imperfections it may have, is nevertheless good. God looked upon all the things that he had made and saw that they were very good. (Cf. Genesis, chapters 1 and 2.) The reality of the complete internal life of God implies that what has existence besides God is related to this perfect life of God as *not* needed by God. Or, to state the same idea more positively, God freely chooses to create what is not himself. All else stands related to God under the aspect of freedom and gift, not of necessity and requirement. Moreover, what is created freely outside God is imperfect when compared to God. There cannot be two Gods. The importance of beginning with this notion is to dispel at the start any notion that imper-

fection and weakness are necessarily equated with evil. The
cosmos and created reality within it are changeable and imperfect, but they are still good. It is good to be imperfect.
For a creature, it is good not to be God. This is essentially
what the first chapters of Genesis are about.

Whatever exists besides God exists because of the life of
God, that is, because of the trinitarian life. The cause of creation, then, does not lie in creation itself but in God. Creation
is shot through with the mystery of the divine choice. And
this is not meant in any merely mystical or a-worldly sense;
in the very fabric of creation itself are found these "vestiges"
of God, since it is in creation that God's choice results and
emerges into being outside himself. There is and must be,
then, an outer limit, as it were, in the investigation of nature
which is caused by the fact that the distinction in things
is primarily the result of God's free choice. This means in
part that there will always be a certain cloudiness in things, a
certain density penetrable only by God, since all reality reflects his choice, which only he can fully comprehend. But
this cloudiness is the obscurity that sheds warmth and light.
It is the invitation to sunshine. This limit is not one of for-
biddenness but one of capacity. The universe is not intended
to be a place where we fear to tread, but merely a place so
immense and wonderful that only God can fully comprehend
it. "How rich are the depths of God—how deep his wisdom
and knowledge—and how impossible to penetrate his motives
or understand his methods! . . . All that exists comes from
him; all is by him and for him. To him be glory for ever!"
(Romans 11:33-36)

Such an approach to reality, then, can recognize that the

principles which govern cosmic evolution and development are not totally opaque to man. There are clouds, but visibility is somehow good. Indeed the whole relation of the cosmos to man seems to be that it is open to the penetration of creative intelligence.[1] That is, nature reveals an order which can be further ordered. Nature can be understood and changed, it can be used. If this is the case, it follows that the cosmos itself appears to be a type of communication of intelligence to intelligence. The cosmos is for man. Of itself, it sets up the possibility and reality of mutual communication in a language proper to the creature man; in a language, that is, that derives its images and concepts from the material world.[2]

The imagery of order when used to discuss nature, however, can easily minimize an aspect of reality—more important still in the realm of persons—which follows directly from the freedom of God's choice implicit in cosmic existence as well as from its very opaqueness. This is the element we have seen in our discussion of the inner life of God. It is the element of surprise. There is a danger of becoming accustomed to the world, failing to recognize how nearly incredible the fact is that the world exists at all. The reality and order of the world are simply of themselves quite unexpected, quite *extra*-ordinary. Every true communication, while falling into some order of history, to be sure, is still in a sense unexpected by the hearer. In other words, in our realization that the cosmos and its structure are open to intelligence, in our recognition that the cosmos is for man, we can easily forget the surprise, the mild shock, that must come to all men when they encounter another intelligence, and therefore another person.

The vast ramifications of this vein of thought require deep

meditation. At first sight, the statement that the cosmos is for man seems preposterous. After all, as we shall presently suggest, the scope, size, and complexity of the cosmos as revealed by modern science would apparently lead to just the opposite conclusion—namely, that the cosmos has very little, if anything, to do with man at all. Man is indeed part of the universe; but surely, it is often objected, not an essential part, let alone its purpose. However, certain observations seem pertinent here. The physical size and complexity of the universe have certainly undermined many of the naive anthropocentric theories upon which much of religious apologetic formerly rested. Yet this very expansion of human awareness about the cosmos, far from reducing our understanding of God, has vastly increased human appreciation of the magnificence and power of God. It has not reduced man to insignificance. God is simply more tremendous, more powerful, than had ever been allowed for by our human constructs of him. In itself, this newer, more adequate appreciation of the cosmos is hardly grounds for dejection.

Furthermore, the vastness of the universe and its intrinsic developmental forces do not necessarily, by themselves, relegate man to insignificance. We should not minimize the dignity of spirit in man by comparing it with time and space, realities of another order. We can, indeed, sum up this line of thought by suggesting that man is the one who gazes at the cosmos and understands what is in it. It is not so the other way around. No one any longer supposes that stars, planets, or other sidereal objects themselves possess intelligence. These spatial objects operate within a framework of "laws" or "regularities" which they themselves do not "create" by their own intelligence. To put it another way, if there is any sort of cosmic order and progressive direction within this order, the physical cosmos itself is the receiver of this sign of intelligence, not its maker.

Man, on the other hand, watches the universe. He is not simply part of it, but an observing part. In this individual and collective effort of the human species to examine the cosmos, the first task is simply to observe it, to understand as perfectly as possible its regularities and paths of change. As this effort becomes more and more sophisticated, man begins to understand how he can use these laws and movements in the universe for his own purposes. Man's experience of the earth has been instructive for him. The earth, which once seemed so mysterious and chaotic, gradually has come under the hand of man; its face has been reshaped for human purposes, so that what continues to exist on earth remains or is improved because of man. The earth lends itself to human purposes. But, so far at least, in the macrocosm, the earth remains what it is, a planet of the sun.

Yet we stand in a moment of history in which the universe itself is beginning to yield the secrets of its order. We do not mean by this to enter the discussion about other intelligences in the universe besides man. Statistically speaking, it is both possible and likely. Theologically speaking, the existence of other races of intelligent, corporeal being certainly cannot be ruled out. However, in view of the nature of the Redemption, it seems more probable that there is only one race of men in the universe, our own. But even were we to discover intelligent beings other than ourselves actually living on some nearby planet, it is a safe assumption that they too are concerned about the order in the cosmos, their place in it, and their ultimate destiny. In that case, the same task of mastering the physical universe would be an effort which men would have in common with races other than men. Thus, if such beings other than men did understand and use this order of the universe in which we all find ourselves together, they too would have to do so according to the operative laws actually at work in the universe shared by all.[3] In other words, the "material" universe always seems to stand passively related to intelligence; that is, it does not think, but it is what is initially thought about. This principle again suggests our original line of approach—namely, that if the cosmos is not itself intelligent but reveals order, and therefore intelligence capable of being grasped and employed by other intelligent beings, then the cosmos is essentially a medium of communication. By being what it is, it is for something.

THE COSMOS AND INTELLIGENCE

The trinitarian life of God involves, as we have seen, an absolute completeness in God such that the relation of God to everything else is based upon perfect "unnecessity." God does not need anything else. From the point of view of beings in the cosmos, this will mean that the intelligible order revealed in the world is itself based upon and conditioned by the purpose of the universe which God has chosen to exist.[4] Since the primary choice of all God's activity refers to his own inner life, which is itself a life of total communication of the divine being, it will follow that any communication of divine reality will require a recipient capable of receiving this

communication. And this recipient will not be God, since
life and communication are already complete in God before
the question of the universe arises.[5] (This is why we cannot
conceive of God as being primarily concerned with the universe itself in his essential activity, for that would mean that
God's prime activity was concerned with not-God. In other
words, it would mean that God lacked something in himself.)

The reality of the cosmos, therefore, will be conditioned
by this mediational aspect of the world as something standing
between intelligences. This, of course, is the word and image
theology of John and Paul. (Cf. Wisdom, chapter 13, John,
chapter 1, Colossians, chapter 1.) All things are made in the
image of the Son who is the Word of the Father. The Son
possesses the divine nature as begotten; therefore, as the perfect reflection of the Father. This means that all things created
in the image of the Son reflect in their own way the Father, as
does the Son. Thus, when mankind is said to be adopted by
the Father, its members properly assume the image of the Son.
(Galatians 4:6–7; Romans 8:15–17) All things, therefore,
created in the image of the Son are joined to those who are
brothers of Christ and heirs of the Father.[6] It is in this sense
that the notion of all things being for man reveals a great
depth of penetration. It really is true that created realities
outside man receive their natural orientation to God through
men who can call God "Father" because of the Son who is the
Word of the Father and the image of all things.[7] All creation
including man himself is adopted through Christ into the life
of God. Christ is God. But man and creation never become
themselves God, never form a "hypostatic union" with God
as does the Son.[8] Man and, through him, the creation are

adopted by the Father. The importance of this is that it is the only basis on which creation and human life can retain their status as gifts from God, which is their essential glory. It is good for creation not to become God.

The realities outside God are *for* man who is, in the Redemption, related to the Father as a son. Such a view presupposes that man is part of nature also. All things are created in the image of the Word who became flesh, that is, part of the universe. Therefore, we can derive this principle from the very vastness of the cosmos, namely, that the "wordness" of all things, all things as seen in their communication aspect of standing between intelligence and intelligence, requires the collective effort of the whole species of man in time to be realized in Christ. Theologically, Christ plus all other men equal one man before the Father to whom they return all things in the Spirit as a gift. (Cf. Romans 5:15–21.)

Each individual man, of course, is intelligent, he has a drive to "know all things." But his capacities are limited by time, space, and power. Consequently, we can expect that the relation of communication between God and all things will relate to intelligence socially, just as God's internal nature relates to itself in three persons. The task of ordering the word-oriented creation so that it fulfills its essential function of glory and service will be social. This means that this reflection of the divine will in creation will realize itself in man's total efforts in Christ, the image. The vocation of man with respect to the cosmos is to know the communication that was placed in it by its creator. This is a social effort and an effect of order, since creation is for man, both for his immediate use and for his reflective insight into all reality. The cosmos, therefore, fulfills its mission only by being penetrated by both God's and man's intelligence in such a way that it is able to complete its function of mediation.

The gradual unfolding of the mystery of space and time is, consequently, part of the overall vocation of man in the universe. Compared to the size and life-span of any given man, the proportions of the universe are incredibly vast, though, seemingly, what prevents man from knowing all this is not so much his desire or his personal capacity as his death—a problem to which we shall return in a later chapter. But the universe faces man as a whole species, as a society which remembers and which promises. The fact that eons of cosmic time and light-years of sidereal space are required to support, produce, and sustain man is not of itself an argument for man's insignificance. What is important about cosmic reality is its order and structure, which can be more and more penetrated by human intelligence. Man does not wish to be the cosmos—not a star nor a mountain nor an ocean. He desires rather to behold and to understand these things, to order further their meaning, to be somehow with them.

THE SIZE OF THE UNIVERSE AND RELIGION

The astronomical statistics indicating the insignificance of man in the universe are impressive. Man occupies Planet Number Three of a quite obscure star which is located some thirty thousand light years from the center of the galaxy. In our galaxy, some ten billion stars exist, while one hundred thousand million billion appears to be a conservative estimate for the number of stars in the whole universe. The enormous number of stars in the cosmos has quite understandably prompted scientists to propose that many other suns besides our own have civilizations on planets revolving around them, though no planetary system other than ours has yet been discovered. Some scientists suggest that one in three million stars has a civilization on one of its satellites. Obviously, this would make quite a few civilizations scattered about in the universe.

Such observations, together with time estimates which drive the age of the earth back five billion years, the sun to ten billion, some elements in the galaxy to twenty billion, and the universe itself to twenty-seven billion years, startlingly emphasize the problems associated with a religion like Christianity, which holds that the universe itself was created by God for man (and apparently not too long ago for those with fundamentalist leanings). Many scholars are frankly willing to "face the facts" and admit man's relative nothingness. A powerful trend in atheist humanism has always maintained that man's nobility lies precisely in his rejection of theological myths and his consequent affirmation of man's true position in the universe. He who humbles himself shall be humbled indeed. From this iconoclastic viewpoint, cosmological and biological evolution have dashed all our grandiose hopes, we now know the nothingness from whence we came and whither we are destined. This Promethean fate should be enough for man.

The probability of other civilizations in the universe, however, is not one which man can or should ignore. A whole conference at the Naval Observatory at Green Bank, West Virginia, not untypical of others held elsewhere in the world, was devoted exclusively to the possibility of getting into contact with such other civilizations.[9] Statistical projections based on the age of the universe, the number of stars with planets, and the progress of evolution easily conclude that some advanced civilizations, having evolved enough to solve their problems of warfare, disease, and hunger, are directing their energies to communicating with other worlds like our own. This may not be as improbable as it at first sounds, since both radio astronomy and optical lasers can be constructed right now for sending information enormous distances into space. Assuming a relatively large number of intelligent planetary cultures, getting into contact with one of them is not improbable statistically. Professor Otto Struve, one of the pioneers in this area, points up the implications of this analysis:

> Since we believe we must say "no" to the question: Are we alone in the universe? we must also incorporate within our scientific theories the inevitable conclusion that not only biogenic effects upon dead matter, but also the free will of thinking, living beings can produce observable phenomena in the cosmos. . . . We can no longer take for granted that all observable phenomena are ruled exclusively by what we call the "laws of nature."[10]

The practical probability of our civilization as such ever physically reaching out much beyond Mars, the Moon, the asteroids, and possibly Venus in our solar system is, however, quite remote. The astronomical logistics of the trip are simply too great, even granting the technological development of something like a photon rocket, needed to make the effort feasible.

These efforts to make the universe further known to man,

to take cognizance of its size and content, do have a relevance to Christianity. Much of what the scientists tell us is still theory and speculation, though we are not always told this. But not all of it obviously is mere fantasy. Christianity has always claimed that it could and would accept all truth, no matter from what source, since its doctrines and the conclusions of science ultimately stem from the same source which cannot contradict itself.[11] Yet the changing postulates and conclusions of science have seriously discredited the security of religious doctrine in the eyes of many of our contemporaries. Historically, in fact, a rather close connection between the development of astronomy and the fortunes of religion can be readily documented.[12] Unmoved movers, spheres, separated intelligences, mechanical worlds, motions of celestial bodies, theories of relativity have forced the modification of numerous prevailing views about the nature of the universe.

The upshot of this long record of scientific advance has been especially serious in the sphere of religion. The genesis of religion lies in creation narratives which have been modeled on the beliefs of the eras in which the stories first appeared. Consequently, the gradual elimination of mythological creation stories as actual reports of what happened naturally called into question the whole message believed to be contained in the religion. Christianity is not the only religion to suffer this fate; the same thing is happening to every religion in Asia and Africa today. But what primarily interests us here is Christianity, since it must accept the truths of the natural order as a part of its very structure.

Anthropologists and other historians of culture have observed that religion has frequently served as a means to explain the mysteries of nature to unscientific peoples. Once these mysteries were understood—the rain, thunder, sunrise, electricity—the place and prestige of religion gradually receded, until today among scientific peoples no one would think of looking to religion for theories about the nature and structure of the physical world. Even for such questions as the immortality of the soul, surely a religious issue in some sense, ordinary people are more often than not inclined to turn to scientists for an answer. In the context of all these scientific surroundings, Christianity often feels itself sadly out-of-date, in great need of "demythologizing," to use Rudolf Bultmann's famous term. How can the creation narratives, the Ascension, the primacy of man in the universe, even God himself have any relevance or intelligibility in the modern view of the cosmos? In other words, Is man still pertinent? Is the cosmos "for man" in any meaningful sense, as Christianity is still committed to hold?

SPIRIT AND SIZE

To retain our balance in the midst of such doubts, we need above all to keep a sense of perspective. By all standards of macrocosmic measurement either of time or of space, man is indeed insignificant. This is most obvious. Yet to lose heart and hope over such knowledge is foolish. Twenty billion years of being a rock, or an ion, or even a galaxy is not really an impressive record. We are, to repeat, looking at the stars; they are not looking at us. "I do not believe in dwelling upon the distances that are supposed to dwarf the world," Chesterton wrote in *The Everlasting Man.* "I think there is even something a trifle vulgar about the idea of trying to rebuke the spirit by size."[13] This is exactly the point. We must not chastise the spirit by size. Man, even on his physical and biological side, is apparently as complex as the universe. The thoughts, words, and deeds of man of which religion speaks are as numerous and as infinite as the heavens. Moreover, as Professor R. A. Lyttleton of Cambridge has remarked, "it may be that life and the universe have always existed to- gether; certainly it needs the former to appreciate the latter."[14] We need life to appreciate the universe.

All scientific theories today admit a definite development in the universe at least according to some statistical order. The origins of this evolution are hypothesized in three "rival theories of cosmology": from continually created matter; from an electrical-charge principle in the atomic structure; or (the relativist theory) from an original explosion which sent the parts of the cosmos into the patterns we now observe.[15] Philosophical and scientific theories attacking final causality have done much to discredit this basic concept. However, scientists are beginning to recognize that some irreducible order does seem to operate in the universe. As an indication of this, Professor Werner Heisenberg points to the constants in the equations of matter such as the velocity of light, Planck's action quantum, and some universal length of ap- proximately $10-13$ cm.[16] After listing several other similar constants, Professor Lyttleton adds, "Can they be pure chance? Physicists do not think so, and the consensus of opinion has long been that they are some profound clue to the relation of the atom to the universe."[17]

The mutations and patterns of energy formation in the

more than thirty known atomic particles reveal a predictable order such that one modification flows into another, not simply haphazardly, but in a mathematically described pattern. Arbitrariness and "uncertainty" may exist for "individual" particles, if such entities can be so spoken of, but not for the statistical whole. And the mind is able to grasp this order; often to modify and use it. Thus, the cosmos is reached by man through his science, which stands between him and the universe. In the words of Heisenberg, "the science of nature does not deal with nature itself, but in fact with the science of nature as man thinks and describes it."[18] In spite of its vastness and complexity, therefore, the cosmos is open to man in some real sense. Life, intelligent life, is needed to observe it. The universe itself appears to demand this.

When we turn to the perplexing but legitimate questions, Why is there something, rather than nothing? Where did the matter which inaugurated the whole cosmic development come from? we are left with two alternatives. On the one hand, we can deny any initial relationship between the order of the universe and intelligence. The question of source thus becomes meaningless. Intelligence is merely an accident, an isolated, freakish phenomenon. In such a view, the evident fact that thinking beings like ourselves do exist is wholly "chancy," unconnected with the universe itself. The cosmos is thus what the Greeks called "chaos," something utterly without order. On the other hand, it is impossible to maintain that the origins of matter come from "nothing" defined as no God and no previous substrate of any sort. Some solid-state theorists attempt to minimize this problem by positing very minute creations, one atom of hydrogen in an area about the size of an ordinary living room every few million years. But the problem is the same whether we talk about one atom or about the whole universe.

Some essential relationship, then, between intelligence and the discovered, operating order in the cosmos is not lightly to be set aside as an absurd hypothesis. The point is important. If the evolution and development of the universe does reveal some kind of constant and regular order in its temporal and spatial progress, then to find some connection between the source of order in the universe and man, who is beginning to grasp this order remarkably well, becomes a reasonable position. The history of thought warns us, of course, not to place belief in God in jeopardy by basing it on the latest scientific theories, which might easily be overthrown, and with them, belief in God. Yet man is more and more able to understand and use the very principles which light the sun and the stars. He recognizes their order. The cosmos, therefore, can quite justly be seen as a medium of intelligence, a way by which one kind of intelligence communicates with another in some fashion. Or, to put it another way, the development of man may well be the end of the universe taken as a physical reality. The cosmos can, logically, be seen as a medium by which intelligence speaks to intelligence.

Professor Max Born has suggested that the era of history now opening to man is unique precisely because the human race has within its grasp the knowledge of how to reproduce and to tap the sources of cosmic power and energy.[19] Mankind is no longer limited to his own physical power, to animal power, or to the power of the sun stored in coal, or oil, or water. This knowledge can give to man a kind of material infinity circumscribed ultimately only by the cosmos itself and its destiny. We should not miss the import of this view. To be a man is to have an openness to the universe. This is really what distinguishes man in creation. Man's mind seeks to grasp the unity and order of the entire cosmic system. Now this quest for the mind's mastery of order corresponds with the conclusions of philosophy about the proper object of man's intellect; namely, the order, the structure, existing in material things—all material things. Man here again is defined by his openness to the whole of creation. And this "openness" is something man's mind is "capable of," something which implies that the task of man as man is to use his mind to know this order before him in truth and humility. The Christian presuppositions, then, do make contact with what man has learned about the universe. In the end, the spirit is not dwarfed by matter; the cosmos, in some real sense, is for man.

MAN AND THE COSMOS BEFORE GOD

Christianity and Judaism accept the fact of a revelation by God to man. The God of revelation is a transcendent God, in no way immanent in the cosmos or a part of it. Nevertheless, he is the God who did create precisely this universe, all of it. The origin of something was not nothing but God. The universe of faith and the universe of reason are the same universe known in different ways. Christianity rises or falls on this truth that the same universe to which man is open by knowledge is related to God, the Christian God, the triune

God whose internal life is, with its irreversible order of Father, Son, and Spirit, ultimately the source of all order.

Man knows something is addressed to him by God only if the order of the universe is altered sufficiently to draw his attention to the new revelation. Two immediate problems will arise out of this affirmation, both of which are connected with the language biblical revelation uses to describe God's acts. The first difficulty lies in the fact that the universe is staggeringly larger and older than the Bible envisions, a problem we have already touched on in another context. The second is that the universe contains its own developmental principles, quite unlike biblical concepts. The Christian confrontation with the universe has generally been considered to be weakened during the past several hundred years by its reliance on biblical constructs which alienated it from scientific facts.[20]

However, if we take seriously what modern biblical exegetes have clearly established, namely, that the casting of the creation and redemption narratives in ancient languages and concepts has not imperiled the essence of that divine communication to man, then we can perhaps take a closer look at this revelation to see that there is actually a cosmic vision in the word of God itself. (Cf. Romans 1:18–21; Ephesians 1:3–14; Colossians 1:15–20.) Genesis relates that the world was created for man but became alien to man because of a sin which involved the whole race. The harmony between God, man and the universe was broken by man. God's overall purpose in creation was his intention to associate intelligent beings with himself in his trinitarian life.[21] This purpose never changed, though its mode of accomplishment did as a result of sin. Into the original order of creation, God's plan of redemption was inaugurated to complete God's original purpose in creation. This hope for the New Law, for the Redemption, was always present in Jewish revelation, in God's guidance of his people.

The coming of Christ, the Son of the Father, brought a new law, the law of the inner life of God, of charity, by which men were to live and, through them, creation. The work of Christ was to take the life of fallen man and restore and elevate it to the life of God. Through the resurrection of the body, man, in whom the universe was summed up, was himself to live God's life as an adopted son of the Father in Christ, who recapitulated all creation in himself. In his renewal of creation, in this new life, all of reality was to be associated, a new heaven and a new earth. (Cf. Revelation, chapter 21.) In Christ the beginning and the end are united. Paul tells us in Colossians and Ephesians that Christ is the image of the Father, the firstborn of creation, he on whom all creation is modeled. The order of creation is related to the Son. The Son is the one in whose image the universe was both created and re-created.

The return of Christ, who was the God-man sharing man's destiny, to the Father through his death and resurrection restored the human to the divine, and, as Paul says in Romans, the cosmos was thereby redeemed. (Romans 8:18–30; Hebrews 9) Death and suffering were conquered, not by being abolished but by being accepted and overcome. The work of the triune God thus remains. This is the task of bringing all men to salvation, to associate men with the trinitarian life.

The "groaning" of creation for a new life is, in Christian thought, intimately connected with the destiny of man. Creation is for man. The natural destiny of man as an individual in the cosmos, his desire to know all reality, thus seems to fuse into his communication with God through whom all things were made.

Man is the creature that knows by knowing the universe. He knows God first through the universe.[22] Indeed, with the coming of Christ, man knows God through the Son. No one knows the Father except the Son, who as the Word is the image of all creation and as man is part of the cosmos itself. (John 6:46) The divinity, the cosmos, and humanity all converge on Christ, the Son of the living God. In this sense, creation is "good," as Genesis affirmed. The vocation of the cosmos is entirely related to the rational creature. The size of the universe is not greater than the capacity of man to know it. Indeed, the universe is the testing ground for man. When man defies God, he does so, and he can only do so, by replacing God with himself as the real cause of the knowledge and order in the universe. Such is the way Christianity defines pride, the ultimate sin. The unity of modern thought can, in one sense, be described as an effort to test precisely this thesis about the possibility of man's becoming the sole creator of reality.

For a time it was believed that the universe evidenced no signs of mind. This position is no longer wholly tenable. Yet man's ability to grasp the order of intelligibility in the world unfailingly brings with it the temptation to conclude that this knowledge gives him absolute dominion over the cosmos. And, in a way, this is true. The universe is for man. But the growth in the scope of man's knowledge has more and more resulted not in increased humility and awe, but in increased pride of power, in the astonishing conviction that man is himself the cause of the order in the universe.

As a matter of fact, however, the gulf between this pride and the New Testament concept of man's position in the cosmos is, paradoxically, not as deep as might be expected. Paul never hesitated to tell Christians "All things are yours." The cosmos is, in the Christian view, for man—a position which pride also readily accepts. The difference lies not in the exaltation of man in the universe as in the willingness (or the unwillingness) to accept the cosmos itself as "from another," as a gift freely and lovingly bestowed on man, a gift which he must receive in silence and reverence. Christianity would maintain, therefore, that before man can accept the revelation of God's trinitarian life as a gift freely and lovingly offered to him, he must first accept the universe itself as a gift. The universe is something for man to know and to use, but it is his as something given to him, as something he receives. We have seen that because of the completeness of the inner life of the Trinity, the universe exists as something free and as something chosen. We see more clearly now that it is chosen as a gift to the rational creature. The fundamental problem of man, therefore, is his capacity to accept this astounding creation as something chosen and given to him freely, as an invitation to live ultimately the life of the triune God, the destiny to which God calls man across the pathways of the world.

Christianity is a missionary religion. It never hesitates to order nature for man's purposes, to use the riches of the world for man. But Christianity recognizes that the use of the earth and the cosmos is itself intended to mediate man's relations between man and man as well as between man and God. In facing the cosmos, man eventually comes to know it, then to use it. This knowing and using, however, are always mediated by other men, so that man's highest experience lies in the discovery of other persons. The fact of personality in the universe, then, unifies it. The unique fact of the Christian view of the world is that Christ unites all persons to himself as well as to the universe. Through Christ, men and the world return to the Father. This is true equally in the order of nature, of history, of knowledge, and of activity.

In conclusion, therefore, the impact of theories about the expanding universe must not lead us to minimize the centrality of man in this whole structure. Christianity has within itself a powerful and significant cosmic view that is basic to it. We have been too much inclined to neglect this element because its description in revelation was set down in ancient formulas. Yet it is there. And, strikingly enough, the realization of the vastness and complexity of the cosmos increases rather than decreases our appreciation of the content of revelation. That the universe is infinitely larger and older than earlier interpretations understood it to be is not an argument against the essential meaning Christianity gives to it. Quite the opposite is true. The unity of the universe, its seeming limitlessness, its relation to man and to God are not questions Christianity is less capable of confronting today. The Christian God is the beginning and the end. Our knowledge, as it grows, makes this truth more, not less, believable. The cosmos and Christianity do, in the end, belong together.

NOTES

1. Cf. Gerald A. McCool, "The Philosophy of the Human Person in Karl Rahner's Theology," *Theological Studies*, 22 (December 1961), pp. 537–562.

2. Cf. Thomas Aquinas, *Summa Theologica*, I, 85, 1.

3. The famous novel of C. S. Lewis, *Out of the Silent Planet*, is built on the hypothesis of other orders of salvation for rational creatures not subject to the original sin.

4. Cf. Thomas Aquinas, *De Potentia*, 5, 4–10.

5. Cf. Denzinger, nos. 285, 800.

6. Should there be other beings in the universe, then, there would be at least this common sharing in the same world and communication in it, even though different final destinies might possibly be diverse.

7. Cf. John H. Wright, "The Consummation of the Universe in Christ," *Gregorianum*, 39 (1958), pp. 258–294.

8. Cf. Denzinger, no. 3023.

9. Reported in *The New York Times*, February 4, 1962.

10. Otto Struve in *The New York Times*, December 6, 1959.

11. Cf. Denzinger, nos. 1789–1790.

12. Cf. Alexander Koyré, *From the Closed World to the Infinite Universe* (New York: Harper Torchbooks, 1957).

13. G. K. Chesterton, *The Everlasting Man* (Garden City, N.Y.: Image, 1955), p. 21.

14. R. A. Lyttleton, "The Birth of Worlds," *The Saturday Evening Post*, December 21, 1961, p. 57.

15. W. B. Bonnor, R. A. Lyttleton, and H. Bondi, *Rival Theories of Cosmology* (London: Oxford University Press, 1960).

16. Werner Heisenberg, "Planck's Discovery and the Philosophical Problems of Atomic Physics," in H. Heisenberg, Max Born, Erwin Schrodinger, and Pierre Auger, *On Modern Physics* (New York: Clarkson N. Potter, 1961), p. 17.

17. R. A. Lyttleton, "An Electric Universe?" in *Rival Theories of Cosmology*, p. 31. Cf. also E. L. Mascall, *The Secularization of Christianity* (New York: Holt, 1966), passim.

18. Heisenberg, *op cit.*, p. 12.

19. Max Born, "Reflections of a European Man of Science," in *On Modern Physics*, pp. 57–78.

20. Cf. Rudolf Bultmann and Karl Jaspers, *Myth and Christianity* (New York: Noonday, 1957), pp. 56–71.

21. Cf. "Dogmatic Constitution on the Church," *The Documents of Vatican II*, ed. Walter Abbott, no. 2, p. 15.

22. Cf. Wisdom 13; Denzinger, nos. 1782–1784.

5
Protestantism and Atheism: God Is in the World

The world man lives in, the world that is for man, finds him seeking to discover in his literature and philosophy a meaning for himself and his earthly environment. Christian man is a redeemed man. God has dwelt among his kind. Yet it is not always so clear to the man of today just what it means for God to have chosen actually to enter time, to have actually become a part of human history. It often seems much easier, much more reasonable, to sever any connection between God and the things of the actual world. This tendency to exclude God from any presence in the world can be either religious or anti-religious, as we hope to see presently. What is important here is to remember that ultimately the Christian, if he is to be loyal to his faith, must recognize that somewhere in the context of the world there is a place for the presence of God. "I am not asking you to remove them from the world, but to protect them. . . ." (John 17:15) Christians must understand that the society in the world to come, to which they are called, does begin in the contingencies of time, in this world.

The world was created by God because he chose to invite other persons to live his eternal life: "Father, the hour has come: glorify your Son so that your Son may glorify you; and, through the power over all mankind that you have given him, let him give eternal life to all those you have entrusted to him." (John 17:1–2) It is, therefore, a place where persons created by God exercise their freedom and hence establish their destiny. The world, as we saw in the foregoing chapter, is a medium, a ground for communication between intelligences. It is, as we pointed out in discussing modern literature and society, where man discovers God and where God seeks man. This discovering and seeking have their histories, their agonies, among men. The central position which the world occupies can be seen with special clarity through the contrasting problems it provokes in the history of thought. To see how crucial the world really is for Christianity, a consideration of the convergence of Protestant and atheist thought about the world is most instructive.[1]

The interrelation of historical movements remains one of the most perplexing areas of human thought. The proposition that one idea or cast of mind can and often does generate another is surely too obvious to require much proof. Ideas and whole intellectual systems, to be sure, are static in one very real sense: the essential structure of man's thought becomes fixed once it is uttered in the world. Once Socrates has sat down, the affirmation that he has sat down is fixed eternally. This observation from Aristotle is pertinent. Certainly a man can always change his mind until his very death, but once his utterance becomes public in his speech or writing, it becomes fixed alongside other statements of his. Accordingly, it enters the history of ideas somehow apart from the man himself.

Yet no idea exists outside a mind. Only in an intellect does an idea live and grow. Once a thought has been passed on in that still mysterious process whereby one man teaches another, the idea again sheds its rigidity, as it were, to take up a new spirit, a new incarnation. No longer static, it breathes in new environments and relationships. This is the way one idea grows into another. This is how we can talk about the historical origins of any intellectual movement. The analogy of thought to the growth of living things, however, while containing much validity, has its drawbacks. A seed must grow into a tree, a fetus into a man. Etienne Gilson, in his remarkable book *The Unity of Philosophical Experience*, observed that we are free to accept this or that set of propositions, but once certain assumptions are accepted as operative, we are no longer free to think as we may, but only as we can.[2] Our presuppositions govern, in some sense, the directions in which we can go. The human mind, however, is not always as consistent as it might be, nor can we always perceive ahead of time just where ideas may or may not lead. When the mind does have alternatives before it arising out of the same intellectual sources, the person will not go where he does not choose to go, even though logically he could choose either alternative.

When we look at the history of thought, ranging from Scotus, Occam, Bacon, and Biel, to Luther and Calvin, to Descartes, to absolutism, idealism, and communism, and then atheism, we may very easily suspect that some connection exists here, that the Reformation as arising from nominalism is somehow a prelude to modern atheism. Indeed, this is a rather common and respected position among scholars of history, philosophy, and theology. What truth can be found in this hypothesis, however, is most difficult to assess. After all, it is quite plausible to argue that we can arrive at modern atheism via the path which leads from Aristotle and the Stoics to Aquinas; from the belief in the empirical order of the world to science; thence to a denial that anything outside the limits of the cosmos needs to be posited to account for what goes on within its vast confines. Should this line of thought be valid, Catholicism would appear to be more guilty of establishing this path than Protestantism, especially when we recall Luther's well-known aversion for Aristotle. Historically Protestantism has always stood on the side of God against the assumption that the intrinsic intelligibility of the world provided a way to God. Therefore, Protestantism can preserve its belief in God when what has been learned about the world appears to lead elsewhere.

Before analyzing in more detail the trends in atheism and Protestantism which define their characteristics more particularly, it is perhaps well to attempt a preliminary statement of the main issue involved in treating these two intellectual phenomena together. The question must be asked whether there is here any logical connection of ideas at issue. Is there a common intellectual source in Protestantism and atheism? As we shall see, there is no strict necessity here. But there is an attitude, an intellectual structure, common to Protestantism and atheism which allows their association in so far as they agree. In this sense, it is not too surprising that the "death of God" has recently come to our notice from sources in Protestant theology.

The common intellectual root, to state it in a preliminary fashion, is a profound agreement that there is nothing of God in the world, that all physical and human realities are themselves finite, they disclose only what they are, which is not God. The other side of this question can be stated equally clearly; namely, Can God be so great as to incorporate both the finite and the infinite, both the universe of things and of man, into his plan and yet remain the transcendent God? Can such a God, manifesting himself as so concerned with and related to the world, yet remain at peace with himself in his trinitarian life, finding no necessity to create at all or to have a world outside himself? Indeed, perhaps what we are ultimately asking is whether the Incarnation is possible.

Here, as we seek further to comprehend the Christian vision of the world, it is of great value to pursue the meditative and profound reflections of atheism and Protestantism as they brood upon the finiteness and evil, yet also on the wonder and beauty, of the world of nature and of man. These reflections suggest that atheism and Protestantism each possess what the other lacks and that they both clearly prove that the mind of man cannot rest content either with God alone apart from the world he created or the world alone apart from God. The central reality of the Incarnation, that God became man in the universe, implies that man in thinking about the world and man must recognize both the transcendent God and the sacral world. To neglect either must always end in destroying the world and the man whom God sought to save.

To decide whether there is any intellectual connection between Protestantism and atheism immediately involves the question of the diverse movements within each of these two points of view. Protestantism is quite varied within itself. Atheism contains, if anything, even greater divergencies. Yet these internal disparities are not so great as to render either the term "Protestantism" or the term "atheism" totally meaningless. They both unify a certain train of thought or mode of analysis under relatively common notes by which it is possible to distinguish them. With due recognition of the differences involved, then, some discussion of the similarities and dissimilarities between Protestantism and atheism is possible and helpful in understanding the relation between God, men, society, and the world.

THE PROBLEM OF ATHEISM

Atheism, of course, is found in the Old Testament—"Yes, naturally stupid are all men who have not known God" (Wisdom 13:1)—in some Eastern religions, and in Greek philosophy, especially with the Cynics, Epicureans, and Skeptics.[3] Atheism in Western thought is clearly and closely connected with these great Greek traditions and with their revival in late medieval and early modern philosophy. The problem of skeptical and atheist positions was complicated by the appearance of Christianity, but little doubt remains that its initial modern impetus derived from Greek thought during the Renaissance.[4]

In understanding atheism, however, the most significant question is not where it comes from—that is, from Greek thought, from nominalism, from skeptical relativism caused by the widespread discoveries of other religious beliefs and peoples in the sixteenth and seventeenth centuries, from scientific objections to biblical formulations—but rather what its import is. Indeed, up to the very modern era atheism has been, as the term for the phenomenon suggests, largely negative in character. The weaknesses and anomalies of theistic arguments have been its primary stock in trade. The denial of God was merely a side issue to the main objection that actual theistic and Christian propositions did not square with a general growth in knowledge and experience. Somewhere in the generations that produced Karl Marx and Friedrich Nietzsche—though beginning much earlier with Machiavelli, Hobbes, d'Holbach, Montaigne—a definite change set in whereby atheism became more positive, not so much a polemic against the manifestation of God as a closed system in itself, something not so much against God as for man and for the universe. Behind all modern atheism, whatever its varieties, there is the effort of the human intellect to find some substitute for God as the cause and center of order and intelligibility. And atheism in its highest form is inevitably the effort to replace God by man himself.[5] For the fierce and abiding commitment of the atheist must always be to the world and to man. The suspicion that the world and man are somehow not necessary fills the atheist with horror and scandal. To the Christian, the life of God is sufficient to itself. As we have said, God does not need the world. Yet for any atheist the affirmation that God is sufficient without the world strikes at the very heart of his belief and commitment, since it denies to man any possibility of grasping all reality by himself alone.

The traditional division of atheism into theoretical and practical atheism is often of less value than it might appear. The practical atheist, remaining indifferent to whether or not God exists (or even allowing for the possibility of his existence abstractly), does not really live as if God made any difference. He is content to live on his own terms, God or no God. The theoretical atheist, on the other hand, goes to great pains to deny the very possibility of God's existence. He takes the issue seriously. He believes he knows that God does not exist. But he knows this precisely because he considers that he knows all that does or can exist. Modern theoretical atheism is positive in this sense. Yet even atheists have their commitments, their fundamental interests and undertakings. They do not withdraw from the world or commit suicide.[6] This means in practice that the theist's argument with the atheist is not about God's existence so much as about his definition. What is God? not, Is God? This is true even in the case that man or the world is the absolute. For then the question is whether the definition of God is man or the world. Much of this also applies to the practical atheist. He may be indifferent to the God of religion as he is defined for him, but still his life is lived according to certain very obvious ideals which define for him what he considers reality to be.

THE POINT OF CONTACT BETWEEN
PROTESTANTISM AND ATHEISM

If the argument with the atheist really is "What is God?" rather than "Is God?" then the relationship between atheism and Protestantism can be ascertained. Obviously, no Protestant can, at the same time, be strictly speaking an atheist. Protestants are always believers in God *ex hypothesi*. The atheist will not believe in God, but he will propose an explanation for all that is without God. The question is, then, Is there some correlation between the basic approaches to reality in Protestantism and atheism? John Courtney Murray clearly stated the issue involved:

"For I [quoting J. N. Findlay] am by temperament a Protestant and I tend toward atheism as the purest form of Protestantism." In other words, the religion of modernity, which is Protestantism, is atheist in its logic. The tendency of his Protestant temperament is towards the avoidance of idolatry, but the logic of the tendency . . . there lies the denial of the presence of God. This is biblical atheism. God may indeed be but he cannot be here—in the person of Jesus, or in the institution of the Church. That would be idolatry. . . . In the modern context, he who says to himself, "God is here" is the fool.[7]

The atheist and the Protestant can agree in pointing to any single object in the cosmos, in history, and in the world of men and affirm: "That is surely not God!"

The crucial question about God as it affects both the Protestant and the atheist is really not God at all, but the world of creation. For the atheist, the world and men define all that there is. Such is equivalently the atheist's God. For the Protestant, the world and men define nothing of God. God is something other than all that there is. That it is but a short step from one position to the other is obvious, especially when we reflect that man's capacity for knowledge lies in his cognitive powers which begin and proceed through the world. The reality of God for man depends on the reality of the world. If we posit no avenue from one to the other, the world becomes wholly autonomous for man. And the autonomy of the world is precisely the atheist position. Therefore, the Protestant intellectual attitude to the world which stems from its distrust of the human and finite is logically the godless viewpoint of the atheist who is willing to accept the world at face value. The atheist sees no reason or necessity for any other world but the one that is simply there for man to conquer. The Protestant is in constant danger of yielding this point to the atheist. And yet, reason thinking on the world proceeds beyond it, while the Incarnation sanctified precisely this finite world. Both the atheist and the Protestant again prove that the world is the primary modality under which man becomes aware of God and of himself. For man, the paradox remains true: what he thinks about the meaningfulness of God depends on what he thinks about the meaningfulness of the world. For it is through man's task in the world and his relation to it that God revealed himself to man. If we deny that God has really a task in and through the world for men, as both the atheist and the Protestant are tempted to do, then we end by denying God himself, for it was in this way that he chose to come to man. The conclusion remains true, then, that to defend God we must defend the world, that some fundamental relation does exist, as we have seen, between Christianity and the cosmos.

THE BEGINNINGS OF PROTESTANTISM:
"SOLA FIDES," "SOLI DEO GLORIA"

Martin Luther is certainly the dominant figure in Protestant thought. Luther was haunted by the desire for security before God. Nothing in the current religious practice of his time could set his conscience at ease, neither confession, nor Mass, nor relics, nor devotions. His search for confidence before God led him to Paul, to Romans and Galatians, where he learned that justification before God is not something men acquire by themselves, nor is it a reward for good works; it is the result of a pure gift of God to man. Man must have confidence in God. He must believe that he is saved in Christ despite himself. Man remains a sinner before God, but God does not impute his sins to him. Luther's dialectic led him to stress man's utter inability to be free and sinless by his own power. Unless he is justified by God, he is condemned—that is, he is without grace. The only thing that can save him is his trust in his redemption by Christ. Those who did not share this faith were alone. Those who did formed together a brotherhood, a congregation of worship and praise.

In Luther the beginnings of the Protestant mind are manifest, the principle of authenticity and inwardness before God. Faith alone will save. Whatever external forms of religion might be used, they all needed to be subject to the one truth that we must let God be God, that man's one hope was in his personal trust in God's justification. The structures of hierarchy, sacrifice, vows, sacraments, all were potentially barriers set up between God and man. Man did not need them. In fact, he found them somewhat dangerous since they easily became substitutes for God himself.[8]

John Calvin, too, insisted on justification by faith and grace. God was for Calvin a loving Father who deigned out of his mercy to call some men out of the depths of sin who might otherwise be lost. Human nature by itself was, indeed, corrupt, able to do nothing. But as for those who were once called, they each had eternal security and a particular earthly vocation. They could live a life of moderation together, performing the works assigned to them. The abiding spirit of Calvin, the *soli Deo gloria*, overshadowed all the deeds of men and the whole earth.[9]

In Luther and Calvin we can see clearly the beginnings of the abiding Protestant problem, the problem of what to do with the world. There is hardly any doubt today that a re-emphasis on God, his glory, his transcendence was needed. Indeed, the proliferation of Marian and saints' devotions was itself a reaction to the loss of the idea that Christ was the true mediator before the Father.[10] Luther tended to stress individual man's personal concern before God, Calvin devoted all to God's transcendence. The Lutheran Church in the years following the Reformation break gradually became a state church, while Calvinism, in Geneva and in New England especially, always inclined to theocracy in which the whole of society was ordered to believers. The seventeenth and eighteenth centuries saw great proliferations of Protestant churches and sects, each stressing a different aspect of the Christian message. Some, like the Anabaptists, tended to anarchy, others to chiliasm, others to pietism, to liturgy, to works. The pattern of the Protestant phenomenon became formed. Each group had the right to separate itself from the others according to its own belief from within. Some enjoyed the help of the state, others suffered under it.

THE PROGRESS OF PROTESTANTISM:
IMMANENTISM AND TRANSCENDENCE

Protestantism had been a movement of piety and simplicity, verging often on literalism. Like Catholicism, it was in serious trouble because of state absolutism, and more especially because of the Enlightenment and the rise of science. Religion was becoming less and less respected in the leading circles of the nations. Protestantism had been fortunate in having no Galileo incident, but it faced the problems of the same crisis. Protestantism too needed a restatement of its position in the face of the changing world. A champion was found in Friedrich Schleiermacher. In his *Speeches to the Cultured Despisers of Religion* of 1799, he made the first great intellectually religious attempt to deal with the problem of the relation between God and the world, the intellectual Achilles' heel of classical Protestantism. Luther, to be sure, was quite prepared to admit that works done under justification were the necessary fruit of the New Life in Christ. But the whole Lutheran and Calvinist tendency was, to a very great degree, to hold suspect any admixture of humanity in the worship of the divine. God alone was supreme. John Wesley, to be sure, recognized the significance of the world to Christianity. Christian social concern was always a basic part of the Church he founded. Kant, too, realized the overwhelming import of this challenge of the world to religion. But while Methodism was

strongly influenced by the pietism on which Kant was nurtured, Kant could not follow Wesley's more simple path because Hume had, he felt, effectively challenged the real relation between the world and God. Kant's gigantic effort,
therefore, was precisely to save the reality of God in spite
of the inability of the world to yield a knowledge of him.[11]

Schleiermacher breathed a new spirit. He attempted to
show that God was not so far away after all. "But it is folly,"
he insisted in his First Lecture, "to make a distinction between
this world and the next. Religious persons, at least, know only
one."[12] God does not lie outside man. It is necessary to look
inward:

What can man accomplish that is worth speaking of, either in
life or in art, that does not arise in his own self from the influence
of the sense for the Infinite? . . . What is all science, if not the
existence of things in you, in your reason? What is all art and
culture if not your existence in the things to which you give
measure, form and order? And how can both come to life in
you except in so far as there lives immediately in you the eternal
unity of Reason and Nature, the universal existence of all finite
things in the Infinite?[13]

Religion is based on a sense of dependence, it seeks the unity
of the finite and Infinite. Yet, this relationship between the
finite and the Infinite is founded on fellowship and communication, which is the meaning of the Church. Schleiermacher saw the unity in a conscious communion of humanity,
in the sharing of men.

With this profound sense of the awareness of the Infinite and his lively sensitivity to communion, Schleiermacher is remarkably similar to Feuerbach and to Marx who were shortly to follow him. Of course, both Feuerbach and Marx would deny the whole reality of the infinite except in so far as it was identified in a spiritual sense with the species man. But they both accepted Schleiermacher's notion of communion and participation as basic modes of man's contact with the world. Feuerbach simply denied that God was more than an abstraction of human love and communication. Everything could be explained without a resort to God. Marx elevated the individual approach of Feuerbach to a social and historical level, but he retained the primacy of human sharing as the content of all reality.[14]

For Schleiermacher, it was difficult to maintain the primacy of the transcendent God. During these years of the early nineteenth century, moreover, the Protestant churches themselves became very formal and comfortable. Into this atmosphere was born Kierkegaard. As far as he could see, no one in his era practiced the religion of the New Testament. Kierkegaard believed that before God there were only individual persons. The mob, the crowd, the daily securities of the ordinary Christian's life were really escapes from personality, a sort of despair. Such contented citizens knew nothing of the risk and abandon of the quest for God. For God, all things were possible. All else was absurd. Human calculations and manipulations could never attain to God with certainty. God was the ultimate chance and concern. Abstractions made by men only led to false gods. Humanity could not

save itself. Only by taking the risk, by denying all the comfort and security of the Christian churches, by standing alone
before God could the Christian really meet him.[15]

Schleiermacher and Kierkegaard represent in Protestantism
the two widely opposed tendencies to immanentism and
transcendence. Overstress on the transcendence of God begets a reaction in the direction of the universal presence of
God. But the finding of God in the inmost recesses of the
heart occasions a temptation to transform God into human
concepts and terms. Schleiermacher and Kierkegaard, however, did have one thing in common, their primary concern
for existential communication as the primary relation between
man and God. Schleiermacher to a greater extent than Kierkegaard was able to bring humanity into this interchange.
Kierkegaard was more able to see the unique meaning of the
personal relation between man and God.

THE PROTESTANT CONCERN FOR THE
WORLD: THE RISE OF THE SOCIAL GOSPEL

The alternative between a semi-mystical immanentism and
an equally mystical transcendence leaves the world of ordinary affairs in a somewhat precarious state. But if Kierkegaard
represents one strain in Protestant thought which declines to
accept the mediation of the world before God, Adolf Harnack, following a stream with its source in pietism, Wesley,
and Schleiermacher's notion of the Infinite in the finite, became at the turn of the twentieth century the leader of
liberal Protestantism which sought to deepen the relationship
between Christianity and the world. Harnack inherited and

himself furthered the very development in biblical and historical scholarship in which it was beginning to be seen that the
New Testament itself contained a growth principle, that the
writing of John and Paul were, in part, theological reflections
on a more primitive kerygma, that the Church of the second
and third centuries, the Church of the fourth and fourteenth
centuries, contained new emphases and brought new stresses
in Christianity.

By going back through this history, it seemed possible to
distinguish and weed out all later additions to the pure
message of Jesus. "No! the Christian message is something
simple and sublime, it means one thing and one thing only.
Eternal life in the midst of time, by the strength and under
the eyes of God."[16] The Gospel is religion itself. "In the
combination of these ideas—God the Father, providence, the
position of men as God's children, the infinite value of the
human soul—the whole of the Gospel is expressed."[17] With
Harnack the social question, the Church's concern for the
poor and the weak, again became dominant. Asceticism and
all that was based on a denial of the world were eliminated.
He saw in the Reformation a return to three basic elements in
the religion of Jesus: religious experience was based on the
word of God and faith alone, this experience was directly
founded on God's grace, and worship became the acknowl-
edgement of God as the Father. Everything else was superfluous. The essential Christian message was something everyone could grasp, something of basic simplicity, beauty, and
clarity. "Protestantism reckons . . . upon the Gospel being
something so simple, so divine, and therefore so truly human,
as to be most certain of being understood when it is left

free entirely, and also as to produce essentially the same experiences and convictions in individual souls."[18] The Protestant mind again took the world seriously, but religion even
more so. Religion was sublime, it did not belong to what was
external to it.

The further development of social concern in the liberal
tradition can be seen in Walter Rauschenbusch's Social Gospel. Rauschenbusch realized that the individualist concept of
man before God did not really include a grasp of the importance of society.

> God is not only the spiritual representative of humanity; he is
> identified with it. . . . He works through humanity to realize his
> purposes and our sins block and destroy the reign of God in
> which he might fully realize himself. Therefore our sins against
> the least of our fellowmen in the last resort concern God. There-
> fore, when we retard the progress of mankind, we retard the
> revelation of the glory of God. Our universe is not a despotic
> monarchy, with God above the starry canopy and ourselves
> down here: it is a spiritual commonwealth with God in the midst
> of us.[19]

In this light, Rauschenbusch identified sin with sin against
society. Selfishness was its dominant note. God is concerned
with man: this is what is characteristic of Christianity as
opposed to a pre-Christian religious state. The mystical experience leads to an avoidance of man's problems, and thus
does not add to the growth of God's kingdom. The essential
note of this kingdom is the Christian transformation of the
social order. The catastrophic and eschatological elements of

the Christian message must be put in developmental terms. Rauschenbusch, then, makes a brilliant effort to realign Protestant thinking with the world and its tasks. He sees that no reader of the gospels can for a moment forget the primacy and importance of the world to the Christian.

THE SCANDAL OF THE WORLD: THE RETREAT TO GOD

Disturbed by the manner of coming to terms with the world found in the traditions of Harnack and Rauschenbusch, Karl Barth and Reinhold Niebuhr, in the sobering aftermath of World War I, came to the view that God really could not be immanent in the activities of the world. He could not be identified with any of the movements of time. The God of European and American civilization, Barth preached in 1916, in words that were strangely prophetic, "is an idol. He is dead."[20] God "is not something among other things, but the wholly other, the infinite aggregate of all merely relative others."[21] Here is a reemphasis on Calvin's and Kierkegaard's insight about the transcendence of God. No merely human effort can attain to God, he must come to us. Nothing we can do will ever alter this fact. Man is not good in himself and is powerless of himself to achieve good. Barth will completely deny the concept of religion as the inward awareness of the Infinite in the finite by the finite's own power. This would make Christianity just another species of the genus religion. By themselves, all things are dead. The only life is the wholly Other.

Niebuhr realized that history did not allow men to neglect

the reality of evil in the world. Whatever the social gospel might uphold will be subject in the end to the ravages of man in society, to war, hatred, evil. "Moral man and immoral society" meant for Niebuhr that man always found his institutions subject to the corruptions of the world.

Individual men may be moral in the sense that they are able to consider interests other than their own in determining problems of conduct, and are capable, on occasion, of preferring the advantages of others to their own. . . . But all these achievements are more difficult, if not impossible, for human societies and social groups.[22]

The reconciliation of the Christian to the world, such a hopeful prospect for Niebuhr's teacher Rauschenbusch, was never wholly possible. The judgment and transcendence of God always meant that earthly institutions of their very nature slipped off into corruption.

THE PROTESTANT DILEMMA: HOW TO
ACCEPT THE TRUTH OF CHRIST AND
THE TRUTH OF THE WORLD

If experience demonstrates that the world constantly betrays the Christian, where is he to go? Two solutions are being forged by recent Protestant theology. Rudolf Bultmann and Paul Tillich have proposed a kind of Christian existentialism which enables man to confront the reality of God directly, person to person, as it were.

The later writings of Karl Barth and the work of Emil Brunner, both based on the scriptural insight that the Incarnation really happened, seek to reestablish both the world and God through the person of Jesus. Rudolf Bultmann, on the other hand, adheres to the tradition of Schleiermacher and Harnack, which sought to be faithful to the realities of the world. However, this loyalty led Bultmann to sever the connection between the world of science and that of Scripture, since he felt that the two were simply disparate. The Bible must be "de-mythologized." Man "must recover this deeper meaning behind the mythological conception of Scripture."[23] The true meaning of Jesus' gospel is that security cannot be found in anything that man does. Since the explanations of science are something quite unconnected with Scripture, the true reality lies in faith. "Faith is the abandonment of man's security and the readiness to find security only in the unseen beyond, in God. . . . For in this world, nothing of God and of his activity is visible or can be visible to men who seek security in this world."[24] The relation between God and the person is not through the visible world, which does not comprehend the whole of reality. God belongs to personal existence. The word of God in Scripture is addressed to the person. The search for God revolves around man's problem with his own existence. Indeed, the problem of God and of man's existence are the same problem. God's actions cannot be proved. His word is concrete, addressed to the person here and now.

Man in Christianity, therefore, is defined as will, not in the Greek terms of reason and the cosmos. There is no room for law and miracle. The world cannot be understood as following some divine law. God is not as we conceive him. If we think we understand him, we must know that we cannot ever understand him fully. The result of this stress on the inability of God to be known in any other way but directly, the inadequacy of any part of creation to help man, completely secularizes the world. Yet paradoxically it enables man to believe in God's mastery over it.

> The man who desires to believe in God must know that he has nothing at his own disposal on which to build this faith, that he is, so to speak, in a vacuum. . . . Luther has taught us that there are no holy places in the world, that the world as a whole is indeed a profane place. This is true . . . the whole of nature and history is profane. It is only in the light of the proclaimed word that what has happened or is happening here or there assumes the character of God's action for believers. It is precisely by faith that the world becomes a profane place and is thus restored to its true place as the sphere of man's actions. Nevertheless, the world is God's world and the sphere of God's acting. Therefore, our relation to the world as believers is paradoxical.[25]

We see in Bultmann, then, the abandonment of any relation between the world and God as the precise means of restoring God to man.

Paul Tillich shares this existential concern that is so clear in Bultmann. No external fact or dogma can lead us to God. Who is God, then? "God is the fundamental symbol of what concerns us ultimately."[26] Whenever and wherever we perceive in our depths a concern that transcends our whole being, we have found God. "The name of this infinite and inexhaustible depth and ground of all being is God. The depth is what the word of God means. And if that word has not much meaning for you, translate it and speak of the depths of your life, of the source of your life, of your ultimate concern, of what you take seriously without reservation."[27] Again we see how easy it is for transcendence to pass over into immanence. Tillich puts his stress on an immediate confrontation between man and God. God is man's ultimate concern; hence even the atheist is a believer. Indeed, it is remarkable how in the thought of both Bultmann and Tillich man's need of the world in his pursuit of the Christian God seems to evaporate.

How, in view of all these divergences, are we to divine the elements common to all of Protestant theology? What is its basic spirit? Tillich is of great help here. He has set down what he calls "the Protestant principle," which is indeed an apt statement of what we have been seeing in operation. "No partial loyalty may be transformed into an ultimate object of loyalty; nothing man-made, or less than divine, may be treated as though it were divine."[28] This principle has been seen to evolve in two directions. In Luther, Kierkegaard, and the early Barth, there is an insistence on the utter transcendence of God, on a consciousness of the nothingness of creaturely works before him. In Schleiermacher, Harnack, Rauschenbusch, Bultmann, and Tillich, God is present to each person in faith in the intimacy of his being. God is all in all, more present than the person himself. But this life is a communication and a transformation in which the kingdom becomes present among men. All things are thus transformed by faith, even though, as with Bultmann, it is only an invisible world.

The Protestant principle is undoubtedly the key issue

which brings the intellectual attitude of Protestantism in touch with that of atheism. Again, it is not a question of whether the logic of Protestantism would lead inevitably to atheism. The crucial issue is whether the world of nature and man are so wholly separate from God that the atheist supposition that all that is, is contained in man and the world, that the protest "We do not need this hypothesis!" is practically verified. The Protestant principle tends to undercut the world by separating it from God. If there is no sign of God in the world itself, in that world open to the human intellect and to man's faith as given through the world, then it seems difficult to establish any real connection between man and God. The atheist is the first to accept this very truth. He can open himself to all that is for its own sake, since he rightly sees no need or room for a God who does not approach man through a finite world constituted by men and other finite creatures. But to deliver the finite, sinful, changing world to the atheist is to grant too much, for it is precisely this world that God loved and created for men. Hence, to save belief in God is also to save the world. The Protestant difficulty in accepting the world and its men and institutions as both finite and saved is perhaps Protestantism's greatest obstacle in teaching men about God.

That this problem is being recognized more and more frequently in recent Protestantism is clearly seen in the later Barth and in Emil Brunner. Louis Bouyer, in his book *The Spirit and Forms of Protestantism,* has summed up Barth's earlier problem:

The God of Barth is but the exasperated negation of this negation, disguised as an affirmation. . . . Barth's "faith" is reduced in the end to an affirmation, in complete darkness, of a God who can no more approach man effectively than Kantian man can attain to God in himself. . . . His omnipotent God is prohibited a priori from ever acting outside himself, his creator is forbidden to create, his savior to save anything outside himself.[29]

The Barth of later years, however, has discovered a God who can act and save. "The God of the Gospel is no lonely God, self-sufficient and self-centered. He is no 'absolute' God. . . . To be sure, he has no equal beside himself. . . . On the other hand, he is not imprisoned by his own majesty, as though he were bound to be no more than the personal (or impersonal) 'wholly other.' "[30] God is not just beyond or above man, but for him, he is man's brother and friend. Barth has discovered the "humanity of God." The concept of a God who is "wholly other," while stressing a true aspect of God, is not all. The new approach to God is centered on the Crucifixion. The starting point is still the deity, but from this deity comes God's humanity. It did not seem right to make God great at the cost of men. "We viewed this 'wholly other' in isolation, abstracted and absolutized, and set it over against man . . . in some such fashion that it continually showed greater similarity to the deity of the God of the philosophers than to the deity of the God of Abraham, Isaac, and Jacob."[31]

But God acts in Christ. "In him the fact is once for all established," Barth writes,

that God does not exist without men. It is not as though God stands in need of another as his partner, and in particular of man, in order to be truly God. . . . Why should God not also be able, as eternal love, to be sufficient unto Himself? In his life as Father, Son, and Holy Spirit he would in truth be no lonesome, no egoistical God even without man, yes, even without the created universe. And he must more than ever be not for man; he could —one even thinks must—rather be against him. But that is the mystery in which he meets us in the existence of Jesus Christ. He wants in his freedom actually not to be without man but with him and in the same freedom not against him but for him, and that apart from or even counter to what man deserves.[32]

All the world returns to man in Christ, and with this return, all culture and society. Jesus is the head of the body that contains the men whom God has chosen. In the end, God gives man a task in the world. He gives men their freedom and their being. "God wants man to be his creature. Furthermore, he wants him to be his partner. There is a *causa Dei* in the world. God wants light not darkness. He wants cosmos, not chaos, he wants peace not disorder. . . . Even in this central act, God declines to be alone, without man. God insists on man's participation in his reconciling work."[33] Barth, then, through his profound study of Scripture, has made a brilliant attempt to confront again the world that God has created and saved in Christ.

Emil Brunner has this same basic realization of the need for the world in Christianity. Moreover, this concern is a social concern. "His will is wholly a social will, a will for a people, for a community; therefore God recognizes no service of God which is not at the same time a service of man."[34] Brunner incorporates the concept of creation into revelation. Thus, man's natural knowledge of the world is really a revelation of God's purposes, his orders. God does not intend to draw men out of the world in any mystic sense or ideal manner. Rather, accepting the tremendous meaning of the Incarnation, Brunner sees how intimately the world and God are associated for man. God's will is his own. Yet, in accomplishing his own end, in his love, "he sets up an end outside himself—without ceasing to be his own end; this end is the communion of creatures with himself, the Creator. The divine will for community is God's sovereign will."[35] The created world is not a mere chaos, but has definite forms and principles which man must discover and reverence to understand what God wills for him. Brunner is able to effect a real union between creation and God's majesty through the recognition of God's will in the world freely choosing to draw men to his purposes.

If we carefully examine what Barth and Brunner have done, we shall see that they have been engaged in a valiant endeavor to prevent Protestantism from leading to any form of atheism. They have seen that the Protestant principle really does contain certain implications which can carry the believer completely outside the real world. But by no stretch of the imagination can the Christian God be interpreted as being unconcerned with man in the world and with what man does in the world. Indeed this is a solid criterion of judgment: whenever any idea of God conceives him as unable or unwilling to touch the created cosmos, that view of God is no longer Christian, however exalted it might seem. Moreover, creation itself belongs to the divine purpose. Brunner saw clearly the danger of denying this truth: "We need only think out the idea of absolute dependence on God, of the *sola gratia*, of the *soli Deo gloria*, of the omnipotence of God, to its furthest point logically, and we shall end—as, for instance, we can see in Zwingli's work *De Providentia*—in the very heart of pantheism. If God does everything, then all creaturely independence is an illusion."[36] In so far as the Protestant principle does not allow for a divine purpose in the world, in so far as everything is held in suspicion, Protestantism will always be open to the atheist temptation to believe that man and the world are really sufficient unto themselves. For if God is expelled from the universe in this way he becomes unnecessary to incarnate persons whose openness to reality must always begin with the physical world.

The connection between Protestantism and atheism, as perhaps the work of Hegel himself best exemplifies, centers on the ability of God to associate himself with the finite world while still remaining the Lord of History. If God can do this, then the world will look quite different from either a Protestant or an atheist viewpoint. Without some recognition of the ability of man really to act in the world under God's will and love, Protestantism must end, as Brunner saw, in a denial of the human. And since man cannot for long persist in such a basic rejection of his being, the Protestant can easily slip into the atheist thesis that this world is of fundamental, absolute importance. It is all there is, all that matters, since there is no real place for God in the finite world. This indeed, as we shall see shortly, is precisely the tendency in more recent Protestant theology.

We should not forget, however, that the atheist himself has gone as far as he can go along one line of thought. And while he grasps something that the Protestant principle very much lacks, namely, an appreciation for the world and its tasks, still the atheist in thinking about this world must encounter more and more its finiteness. Finiteness, however, is something that the intellect can never really rest with, so that the atheist in his purest form will himself be constantly tempted by the transfinite, by that which does not bear the limitations he so vitally experiences. What atheism and Protestantism together prove about the nature of the human intellect is that reality must provide a legitimate task for man, a task that is truly meaningful in the earthly sense but that simultaneously leads men to the transcendent God who is beyond and apart from finite limitations.

THE LOGIC OF ATHEISM: THE
SUFFICIENCY OF MAN

It is of some importance to understand why the "salvation of the world"—that is, the recognition of the Christian reality and importance of the world—is such a vital question in the relationship between Protestantism and atheism. The problem arises in essence out of Aristotle. For Aristotle man was the being whose proper activity in the universe combined body and soul. Sense knowledge as the source of intellectual knowledge was what was most characteristic of man. To be a man was to know by the senses. Man did have an intellect which was a higher power, but this was somehow beyond man and divine.[37] In the evolution of atheistic thought, this basic definition of man as the sensuous being whose reality was open to the world was accepted, but the primacy of the theoretic reason over the senses in Aristotle was denied. Emil Brunner's analysis is accurate:

Modern atheism is always connected with a naturalistic psychological theory of religion. This again, in some form or another, is derived from the philosophical doctrine of sensationalism; this naturalist theory also explains away, by its psychological arguments, all those immanent-transcendent ideas of truth, goodness, and perfection. Apart from a naturalist philosophy which derives mind from matter, the atheistic thesis is difficult to prove, unless—as in modern times in Nietzsche and Nikolai Hartman—it appears as "postulatory atheism." "If there were gods, how could I bear not to be a god? Thus there are no gods." (Nietzsche) For the sake of freedom, God must be denied. In this form, atheism betrays its real dynamic idea. Man wills to be master, therefore there can be no other master. This kind of atheism obviously is the lie accepted by the man who refuses to be a creature, but who wills to be absolute.[38]

This point about the primacy of man's composite nature, its all-sufficiency in what pertains to it—politics, economics, social organization as well as science and technology—can be seen most clearly in Marx. For Marx, atheism is a humanism. Following Feuerbach's insights, he saw that the real for man must be the sensuous and socially concrete. "Atheism and communism are not flight or abstraction from, or loss of, the objective world which men have created by the objectification of their faculties. . . . They are rather the first real emergence, the genuine actualization, of man's nature as something real."[39]

Thus the proper object of man's mind is really sensible being. With this realization, Marx launches his attack on God at precisely this point where man is most truly human, in the world proper to man as a composite being. If, therefore, the whole world of nature and society is really nothing but an attempt to humanize this world, then all being is defined by humanity. There is no room for God. The strong point of this position, of course, is that man really does find his being's very structure oriented to the physical world. Any denial of this cannot but seem alien to man.

For Marx, the task of science and labor is to socialize and humanize nature. "The eye has become a human eye when its object has become a human social object, created by man and destined for him."[40] Nature is the objectification of man. This involves all of humanity. But "the individual is a social being."[41] This is the key to Marx in his theory of the species-being of man.

Man is a species-being not only in the sense that he makes the community his object both practically and theoretically, but also in the sense that he treats himself as the present, living species, as a universal and consequently free being. . . . Conscious life activity distinguishes man from the life activity of animals. Only for this reason is he a species-being. Or rather, he is only a self-conscious being, i.e., his own life is an object for him, because he is a species-being.[42]

Marx has actually confused being with logical being. For the whole trend of his system is to subsume man and nature under humanity as the real and perfect being of his philosophy. This means, therefore, that he cannot accept the world and man as being given, prior to humanity. He finds no absolute tendency or direction outside man and the world. Thus the atheism of Marx results precisely from the removal of God as a real cause for the distinction of things in the world. The danger of the Protestant principle lies in its conformity with Marx's view of the world, in its acceptance of the idea that God is not present in the world itself or really relevant to it. Once this is granted, the cause of God seems doomed.

"O my friend," sighed Nietzsche, "man is something that must be overcome."[43] The evolution of European thought and society has gone beyond Marx. The mind is not long satisfied in making a god of humanity. "The greatest recent event— that 'God is dead,' that the belief in the Christian God has ceased to be believable—is even now beginning to cast its first shadows over Europe."[44] The atheism of Marx was humanist, but Nietzsche saw, in terms remarkably similar to Kierkegaard's, that the mob, the life of the common human crowd, could not suffice. Greatness consisted in overcoming such a mass man. The superman had to recognize that all which remained of Christianity had to be replaced. To be a new being by setting oneself off against the crowd became man's goal. And this belief has a metaphysical purport since it means actually creating new being opposed to the only being known in the world. Marx was content to overturn all existing society for the species-being man so that each man was really identified with the species and therefore could participate, indeed, could be all being. Nietzsche protested, "All that you have called the world, that shall be created only by you: your reason, your image, your will, your love shall thus be realized. . . . Evil, I call it, and misanthropic—all this teaching of the One and the Plenum and the Unmoved and the sated and the Permanent. All the permanent—that is only a parable."[45] Atheism, therefore, reaches its ultimate limits in the death of God, in the overcoming of humanity. In a sense, this is the limit of the world without God, the effective replacement of God not by humanity but by the individual. Brunner's observation that atheism is the personification of pride is justified.

"In choosing myself, I choose man," writes Sartre.[46] But can we still convert Nietzsche's aloof and exalted being into man? Nietzsche protested against the mob, against the mass of believers in dead idols. Sartre sees quite well, however, that the attempt to create a new being other than man is a dead-end street. Man is greater, he has more possibilities, than this. Besides, there is nowhere else for the atheist to go but to man if he does not wish to end in sheer nothingness and silence. Nature itself will always yield, on analysis, a certain random unintelligibility alongside some definite signs of order. Since for the atheist the only known source of order in the universe is man, this is the direction in which he must go if he wishes to remain authentic to the world in which he finds himself. For Sartre, this means that existence precedes essence. That is, in the beginning man exists as a void. What he is to be depends solely on himself:

What is meant here by saying that existence precedes essence? It means that, first of all, man exists, turns up, appears on the scene, and only afterwards, defines himself. If man, as the existentialist conceives him, is indefinable, it is because at first he is nothing. Only afterward will he be something, and he himself will have made what he will be. Thus there is no human nature, since there is no God to conceive it. Not only is man what he conceives himself to be, but he is also only what he wills himself to be after this thrust toward existence. Man is nothing else but what he makes of himself.[47]

Man is thus condemned to be free. He finds himself, he must create himself. The problem of God is simply not the issue. What exists is the universe of man and his inner life. The obvious result of this system of thought is simply that man desires to be God. "The best way to conceive of the fundamental project of human reality is to say that man is the being whose project is to be God. . . . To be man means to reach toward being God. Or if you prefer, man fundamentally is the desire to be God."[48] The universe devoid of any *signs* of God in itself leaves man bare and naked, faced with the sole problem of making something more of himself than what he was given. Atheism means, then, the accepting of the power of the human will in a world devoid of any other rational purpose but that which belongs properly to man.

THE SECULARIZATION OF THE WORLD

If there is any outstanding characteristic of the contemporary world, it is the irrepressible drive on the part of all men and nations to transform it, to modernize it by technology and science. No nation, no ideology, no religion can resist this trend. Few indeed even want to try. And though science and technology are, in a sense, universal and can obviously be learned by any man or nation which has the patience and desire to follow the formulas and techniques already learned by others, the fact remains that the origin and driving force of the scientific and technological movement are Western in origin. The spread of this spirit to the rest of the world arises out of Western ideals and ambitions. As Christopher Dawson has perceptively written:

> Nevertheless, it was in the West that the process of secularization began, and Western civilization was the creator of that technological order which is now the real basis of secular culture. Indeed, the Eastern development is due to a great extent to the imitation of Western technological culture, and its violence and intolerance is partly due to its desire to "catch up with" the West and carry through in a generation the changes which took a century or more to develop in the West.[49]

The ideals and demands of this new civilization are sweeping everything before them. The problems this rapid change is causing have given the West a great crisis of conscience because it fears its gift, however well intended, may be the cause of more trouble in the world than it suspected. But it is no longer possible, in any case, to ignore the new world being created before man's very eyes.

For the modern atheist, the creation of this new world for man under the control of man seems only right. Recent Protestant theology, however, suddenly becoming aware of this new phenomenon, has also—unexpectedly, perhaps, but still understandably—revealed the precarious nature of its confrontation with this new world. Indeed, the tentative approaches of Brunner and Barth to the world via the Incarnation have proved inadequate, or at least have failed to appeal to a younger generation of Protestant theologians. The cry of Nietzsche at Rapallo in 1883 that God is dead is beginning to be heard and heeded. We have stated that there is no intrinsic reason why the Protestant should necessarily become an atheist, though it is always a logical possibility. We have suggested that there could be a perennial temptation to follow this path because of the precarious status of the world in classic Protestant thought. It is perhaps a valid principle to affirm, at least on Aristotelian grounds, that if man is given an apparent choice between a god without the world or a world without a god, he will instinctively—and rightly—opt for the latter because he cannot long doubt the concrete reality of ordinary life.

Now something of this sort seems to have been happening in current Protestant theology as witnessed by the celebrated controversies over secularized Christianity and the death of God. Having grasped collectively and with consternation the actual status of religious belief among modern men, Protestant theology, so long concerned with strict biblical studies and categories, with God as wholly other, has found itself unable to resist intellectually the shock of the sudden swing to the world without God, the world of mankind in anguish.[50] Current Protestant theology takes up where modern atheism has left off—with a world which can no longer easily believe that there is still some life in the dry bones of Christianity. In a sense, it is a world beyond the "humanity of God," beyond Barth, Brunner, and even Bultmann. And while the prophet of this world is still a German, Dietrich Bonhoeffer, the disciples are not only German but English and American also. We live in the world of *Honest to God, The Secular Meaning of the Gospel*, and *The Secular City.*

The problem, however, is still the world—the problem of believing that the transcendent God could possibly have associated the finite world with his eternal purposes. In a sense, the *sola Deo gloria* still stands in the background forbidding Christianity to claim any worldly city or person or institution as its own certain witness. The vibrant city of the world, however, can no longer be ignored while Christians read and study the Bible. The glory of man has cast its shadow over the glory of God. Christianity's traditional doctrines seem to have lost most of their significance. The pressing problem this generation faces, then, is every bit as serious, and perhaps of the same order, as the passage of the Gospel from the Hebrew world to the thought patterns of Greece and Rome. We are confronted with the task of learning how to speak to the modern inheritor of the atheist tradition, to the man who, presumably, is no longer capable of hearing the Christian message because Christianity has become itself something of an outmoded idol.

Sola scriptura, sola fides, soli Deo gloria have been the classic Protestant insights. But suddenly we find an acute awareness of the absence of God from the modern world. Everyone imitates the famous Bishop John Robinson in regretfully citing Dietrich Bonhoeffer. "How do we speak . . . in a secular fashion of God?" "God is teaching us," Bonhoeffer continues, "that we must live as men who can get along very well without him."[51] But Dietrich Bonhoeffer, whose profoundly moving letters from a Nazi prison cell are surely among the highest tributes to the human spirit in recent generations, was concerned about God when he realized that religious categories were no longer capable of making him present to modern man. Bonhoeffer denied religion to save God.

"Surely it is not possible," Professor Thomas J. J. Altizer has written, "for any responsible person to think that we can any longer know or experience God in nature, in history, in economic or political arenas, in the laboratory, or in anything which is genuinely modern, whether in thought or in experience. Wherever we turn in our experience, we experience the eclipse or the silence of God. To refuse to accept the death of God is to evade our actual condition. . . ."[52] The death of God was in Nietzsche's time an insight, a prophecy if you will, whereas today it is rather presented as a rigorous, rational conclusion of historical, intellectual analysis.

This death of God analysis begins with the Old Testament which deals with destroying the pagan idols. It began the process of secularization on a vast scale. The mission of Christianity is to carry this through, to its ultimate conclusion—the secularization of all things, the death of God, the birth of man. The Old Testament did two things: it destroyed all the idols, all the images of false gods and it gave the world to man "to subdue." The New Testament continued this process by destroying all human idols. The response of Peter and John is fundamental: "You must judge whether in God's eyes it is right to listen to you and not to God." (Acts 4:19) It is noteworthy that this answer was not addressed to Pilate, the Roman authority, but to "the rulers, elders and scribes . . . meeting in Jerusalem with Annas the high priest, Caiaphas,

Jonathan, Alexander and all the members of the high-priestly families" who had been rash enough to ask of Peter and John where they obtained their authority. (Acts 4:5–6) To Pilate, the Roman authority, the answer of Jesus "secularized" forever all civil power that claimed to be of itself divine: "you would have no power over me . . . if it had not been given you from above. . . ." (John 19:11) Thus, if the essential mission of biblical Christianity is "to destroy the idols," to unseat the divinities as well as the *divi Augusti*, then its continual task is to carry through this process to its conclusion. ". . . The Christianity that we know is the product of almost two thousand years of secularization, for secularization began with Christianity's acceptance of the world, with Christianity's submission to the very reality of the world."[53]

Secularization, of course, has long been a kind of "dirty word" in Christian circles, with most unpleasant connotations. Bishops have written pastoral letters warning about it, preachers have lamented its gains. "Creeping secularism" became the religious counterpart of "creeping socialism." All in vain! "It will do no good," Harvey Cox warns, "to cling to our religious and metaphysical versions of Christianity in the hope that one day religion and metaphysics will once again be back. They are disappearing forever, and that means we can now let go and immerse ourselves in the new world of the secular city."[54] There is no longer any possibility for modern man to discover meaning in the world or in himself from somewhere outside, as it were. There is no "outside." "Secularization places the responsibility for the forging of human values, like the fashioning of political systems, in man's own hands."[55]

But like the destruction of idols and the overthrow of absolute kings, this is an exhilarating, liberating experience.

The modern world is fast becoming a modern city. At one time there were rural areas; space, physical and psychological, existed between the city and the countryside. Today we have only city-dwellers who live more or less in the same block and who at no time are more than the dial of the telephone, the click of the ignition switch, the knob of the television set away. We are all more or less immediately present to one another. To go from Fiumicino Airport into Rome takes longer than the flight from Fiumicino to Orly or Rhein-Main. Moreover, if we do not have something, we almost literally "create it." We are becoming more and more independent of sources of supply, we learn to substitute and to replace. We crossbreed to produce the types of animals and plants we want and need. We "smash" atoms, we create new metals and alloys, new machines, new glasses to see with—even, it seems, new hearts to beat within us.

All of this is the product of a "secularization," a progressive, pragmatic, intelligent grasp of the world man must conquer for himself. And the world, like Mount Everest in the famous apologia, must be conquered simply because "it is there." Indeed we simply refuse to believe that even sickness, evil, and death are permanent. A scientist in a recent magazine article wondered whether the day was not seen coming when we would be under the moral obligation to deep-freeze dead bodies instead of burying or cremating them, since we might someday find out how to resuscitate them. Already babies are conceived from semen frozen for several years. The birth of children from genitors long dead seems a real possibility.

Scientists are even talking of clonal reproduction of human beings, transplantation of most human parts, and complete gestation outside the womb.[56]

And evil, what about evil? We are quite used to the theory that it is mainly a question of environment—change the environment, change the evil. *The Lord of the Flies*, however, seems no longer pertinent. "The touchstone of this post-Christian age," Gabriel Vahanian observed, "is not the attempt to fit evil into a coherent view of the universe, but to eliminate it from the universe. How else could man's dominion over nature and its elements be concretely manifested? Man is now what Christ, according to the New Testament, was to the world. He is the redeemer, the meaning-giving center of this post-Christian era."[57] Evil, suffering, death are simply projects to be attacked by organized intelligence, experiment, and technique. We should stop complaining about these things and get to work at removing them.

All of this seems to bear out what Professor E. L. Mascall remarks about Paul van Buren's *The Secular Meaning of the Gospel*, namely, that what we are witnessing is not so much a theology of the secular as a secularization of theology. One of the most remarkable elements in all these studies about the death of God has been the eagerness, the almost frenzied haste, with which many Protestant theologians have felt the need to come to terms with this world. This, of course, is not entirely new, and it is something, if our overall analysis is valid, that we should have expected. Luther himself had something of this spirit in his opposition to the monasteries; the Calvinist tradition of work and duty is well known.[58] Methodism was concerned with works, the Social Gospel movement.

All these trends indicate that Protestant theology has not been fully satisfied with its relationship to the things of this world. What is new in the current trend seems to be that the world is now beginning to teach Christianity what fundamental reality is about, even what Christianity is about—namely, about the world.

Yet there is no question that concern for the world is fundamental to Christianity. When we analyze the reasons why "Come, you blessed of my Father" was addressed to some and not to others, we realize that the test was not primarily one which inquired into the content of belief or the interpretation of Scripture; rather, the question was whether the hungry had been fed, the naked clothed, the thirsty given drink. As we look at the basic international problems which face us today—expanding populations, underdevelopment, poverty, the "third world"—we cannot but be struck by the thought that these are highly sophisticated forms of the needs to which the same salvific criterion applies. The main difference seems to be in the evolution of the corporate complexity and international scope of such problems. In so far as this current mood of Protestant theology, therefore, is founded on this instinctive Christian intuition that the structures of churchly and dogmatic faith and institutions mean little to salvation if they are not found relevant to the earthly task of man, we must rejoice at what is happening. This is, after all, the universal application of the principle of the Good Samaritan, the true vision of who is, in truth, our neighbor. Catholic theology has always felt that Protestant theology has lacked this incarnational confrontation with the world, this sense of a true purpose of God within the realities of time. For all its confusions and exaggerations, this is probably what the controversy about "good works" was about. Without this sense of realistic world relevance, of world charity and generosity, all theology is tinkling brass and sounding cymbals.

THE DILEMMA OF SECULARIZATION

The present question, however, is whether we have to get rid of God to accept the Christian meaning of the world. In a sense, we can be sympathetic to this feeling because of the type of God certain circles of Protestantism have been accustomed to writing about. To protect God from earthly contamination, he had been shunted out of the world by "the Protestant principle," by the fear of trusting any earthly institution, by the hesitation before human arrogance and pride. The trouble is, however, that it is impossible to remain a "christian" and fail to realize that Christianity demands what Karl Barth himself came to call a *"causa Dei"* in the world. There is simply no sense in "believing in Christ" or "in having the faith" if what results from this does not transform man's incarnate environment.

On the other hand, the current uneasiness about God, modern man's supposed inability to believe in any kind of traditional Christian deity, seems to have an intellectual foundation that is highly questionable. Professor Mascall is probably correct when he observes that "the main cause [of man's difficulty in believing] is the continual impact upon the senses of a technocratic culture in which all the emphasis falls upon what man can do with things and hardly any upon what they really are."[59] We have tended to see all mysteries as problems, in Gabriel Marcel's sense, to believe that we really know what a thing is when we know how it works.[60] There is a fundamental truth in this attitude, of course. But it contains an unwarranted presupposition about the nature of the historical evolution that led to the so-called necessity of the denial of God.

This presupposition ultimately has to do with Aristotle. "It is impossible for Western man," Professor Altizer comments, "to disassociate the idea of God from the idea of *Kosmos*, the idea of a rational order which is imbedded in the world. God and kosmos are polar expressions of one root idea: the rationality of the universe, or rather, the very idea of universe itself."[61] The sympathy of Christianity for Aristotle, the great empiricist, is thus supposed to have been the root cause alienating Christianity from science. And Christianity's weakness before science is said to be the basic reason why society is alienated from Christianity today.[62] "Had the Christian church followed Democritus and the atomists instead of Aristotle," Robert Bruce McLaren has observed, "the whole sorry history of conflict between science and religion might have been avoided."[63] Certainly the relationship would have been different, but the pertinence of the otherwise valuable article we have just quoted is lessened by McLaren's assumption that Aristotle was a mere pantheist. This prevented him from seeing how crucial Aristotle was to the whole problem.[64]

Christian theologians have long dwelt on the difference between Greek and Hebrew thought patterns, the destructive rationalism of the Greeks, their lack of a sense of history and of the significance of the person. That there are differences between the two, there is no doubt.[65] But the point at issue here is the remarkable degree to which Greek and biblical thought are in accord with regard to "the very idea of universe itself." The two traditions in fact have been in considerable agreement on the notion that there are not two universes, one for God, another for man and creation. They have agreed that there is order in the universe related to the order in God, that the universe, in addition to being something truly for man to fashion by art and politics and technics, is first something given, first a working unity, first something to behold as from the hand of God.

Thus, in so easily rejecting the idea of cosmos when confronting the world, many Christian thinkers come to conceive the world as in opposition to God because their intellectual presuppositions—whether from Democritus or from the Hebrew-thought comparison—have excluded "the very idea of universe itself." When order is finally imposed on the universe, when man becomes, in Vahanian's accurate phrase, "the meaning-giving center of this post-Christian era," then God is simply set aside as a construct unrequired to explain "how things are" or "how things work."

Dietrich Bonhoeffer wrote briefly on June 8, 1944: "The movement beginning about the thirteenth century . . . towards the autonomy of man (under which head I place the discovery of the laws by which the world lives and manages in science, social and political affairs, art, ethics, and religion) has in our time reached a certain completion. Man has learned to cope with all questions of importance without recourse to God as a working hypothesis."[66] As a matter of fact this movement did not begin in the thirteenth century but with the rejection of the Aristotelian cosmos by the post-Aristotelian philosophers. The thirteenth century saw the beginning of a revival of the ancient argument. In the present-day literature of the death of God we see this controversy reaching its term.

But the important thing here is not so much the historical analysis of this complex evolution which has brought man to autonomy as the idea that God's death is necessary only as an adjunct of a defense—or, better, an exaltation—of the tasks which belong to the world. We should note that there can be a conflict between the notion of God and the concept of a meaning-giving creature only if the possibility of God's creating a rational creature in a universe full of meaning is denied. It is really astonishing that the fact that man has discovered the way things work and what they are should be considered an argument for the denial of God. For in view of the evident fact that man is discovering something already at work in the universe which he did not make but learns by "learning from," it would be far more logical to conclude that he is discovering order, function, and structure which he is imitating, modifying and improving for his own purposes. In short, as we have already seen, man is the creature capable of discovering the signs of intelligence in the order of the world. Hence the fact that man acquires knowledge which he uses for his own mission in the world is in no way in conflict with the idea of God. For God is sufficiently great to create a creature who, like himself, though on a finite level, can know and act, who is free, who has, as Aristotle pointed out, a mind and hands. To save creation, man does not have to destroy God.

At this point in man's development the teaching of Aristotle and Christianity are crucial. For it was Aristotle who warned that if man did not see the difference between the quality of life in the city, where mortal man could fashion his own forms of society, and the life of contemplation, where he realized that the universe itself comes from outside, then he would be tempted to refashion, to revolutionize, the universe on the model of the city—the secular city—so that the order of God would be excluded from the order of man. To this warning of Aristotle's Christianity has added a further clarification: in defining the nature of God's life and his relation to the world of men, in the dogmas of the Trinity and the Incarnation, it has prevented man from seeking to overturn the natural order in his quest for the absolute—in his desire to be all that there is.[67] If man looks on the world—which he did not create—according to the model of the city—which he did create—he can only end up by finding himself alone in the universe.

With the decline of Christianity as an effective force, then, it is hardly surprising that we are again witnessing an effort on man's part to remove the traditional guideposts in the vain attempt to acquire for himself the power over evil, death, and the finiteness to which he is subject. In other words, the desire of man to know all things, the corresponding Christian mission to transform all things in the service of God through man —both perfectly healthy instincts—are being confused with the temptation of man himself to be God, to refuse to acknowledge the gift of the universe that has been made to him, to see that the gifts of life and grace are not from himself but from another even when he is the agent of their relevance in the world. For it is the Christian view that the world is, theologically, for man. Man is ultimately its center.

GOD'S WILL: THE HELP OF OTHERS
IN THE WORLD

When God is dismissed from the cosmos, then, man falls into the classic dilemma of Protestantism, the conflict between loyalty to God and loyalty to the world. The essence of Christianity in the Incarnation is that man must be loyal to both. For this is what man is. He is the mortal who gives meaning to the cosmos because he understands that the cosmos is given to him, given to him to prove his openness to other persons, for whom he is responsible in the world. The secularized world and the death of God are indeed products of the secular city. But as Augustine foresaw long ago, for the secular city to retain its zeal and its sanity about the tasks of man in the world, it must pay some attention to the city of God. The meaning of our time involves nothing less than this.

The relation between Protestantism and atheism, then, must be understood in the context of the logical intuition and interrelation of ideas. In concrete persons, no such necessity exists for Protestantism to evolve into atheism as is sometimes implied, nor is there any necessity for it in the order of the ideas themselves. Whatever might be said against the Protestant thesis, it should be recalled that this much remains primary for it: the worship of the true God in Christ. The way the Protestant principle is applied in the world creates difficulties —serious ones, if our analysis is correct—because it tends towards making God evaporate from the world of man, history, and nature. But this effect is never part of the Protestant intention. The main issue involved in this problem of the relation between Protestantism and atheism can be stated in these terms: How great is God? Is God great enough to associate human persons and institutions, in spite of their weaknesses, in his work in the world? Barth and Brunner form the foundation of an emphasis in Protestantism which sees that leaving God out of the world inevitably results in the growth of atheism. The Christian God manifests himself as someone concerned with the world and men. To fail to realize this is to abandon God under precisely that modality in which he reveals himself to man.

Does the atheist, then, serve any religious purpose? Again Emil Brunner sheds great light on this question: "Indeed there is a permanent truth in atheism, namely, the right to protest against that element of untruth which clings to every human formulation of divine truth, the 'all-too-human' and godless element in theology. Atheism challenges us to recognize that in our hands the divine revelation itself is always mixed with error and arrogance."[68] The Protestant principle is obviously at work here, the constant judgment on all purely human failings. But we must recognize that God is greater, not less, in being able to welcome human, fallible man into association with his divine purpose. God is transcendent; he is also at work among his creatures. The destiny of human beings is the society of the Trinity in which all men share the divine life, in which the world returns to the creator through men. This suggests that the underlying atheist trend placing all possible and visible creation somehow under man is rooted in a basic truth, while the Protestant distrust of all things human also is valid in its emphasis on God's transcendence of the world. But if Aristotle is correct in defining man as precisely the one being in the cosmos oriented to the world, then any true view of God, man, and the world must somehow recognize that these three realities ultimately belong together in harmony, not opposition. This, it seems, is the essential teaching of the New Testament. It is likewise what can be inferred in a negative way from the history of Western atheism and Protestantism, since both have arrived at an impasse in their own order through neglecting this factor of the openness of the world to God and man.

NOTES

1. The importance of both of these subjects is emphasized in Vatican II. Cf. the documents on Ecumenism and The Church in the Modern World, *The Documents of Vatican II.*

2. Cf. Etienne Gilson, *The Unity of Philosophical Experience* (New York: Scribner, 1937).

3. Cf. G. Mensching, "Athesimus, Religionsgeschichtlich," in *Die Religion in Geschichte und Gegenwart* (Tübingen: Mohr, 1957), Vol. I, pp. 670–672.

4. Cf. Ernest Cassirer, *An Assay on Man* (Garden City, N.Y.: Doubleday Anchor, 1944), pp. 15–40.

5. "This future man, whom the scientists tell us they will produce in no more than a hundred years, seems to be possessed by a rebellion against human existence as it has been given, a free gift from nowhere (secularly speaking), which he wishes to exchange as it were, for

something he has made himself." Hannah Arendt, *The Human Condition* (Garden City, N.Y.: Doubleday Anchor, 1959), p. 3.

6. Cf. Albert Camus, *The Rebel*, tr. Anthony Bower (New York: Vintage, 1960).

7. John Courtney Murray "On the Structure of the Problem of God," *Theological Studies*, March 1962, pp. 20–21.

8. Cf. *Martin Luther*, ed. John Dillenberger (Garden City, N.Y.: Doubleday Anchor, 1961).

9. Cf. John Calvin, *On the Christian Faith: Selections* (New York: The Library of the Liberal Arts, 1957).

10. Cf. Godfrey Diekmann, *Come, Let Us Worship* (Baltimore: Helicon, 1961).

11. *Immanuel Kant's Moral and Political Writings*, ed. C. J. Friedrich (New York: The Modern Library, 1949). See especially "Prolegomena to Every Future Metaphysics," pp. 42 ff., 93 ff.; "Critique of Judgement," pp. 363 ff.

12. Friedrich Schleiermacher, *On Religion, Speeches to Its Cultured Despisers*, tr. John Oman. Reprinted with the permission of Harper Torchbooks, Harper & Row, Publishers, Inc., New York.

13. *Ibid.*, p. 39.

14. Cf. Ludwig Feuerbach, *The Essence of Christianity*, tr. George Eliot (New York: Harper Torchbooks, 1957); *Marx's Concept of Man*, ed. Erich Fromm (New York: Frederick Ungar, 1961); *Marx and Engles, Basic Writings on Politics and Philosophy*, ed. Lewis S. Feuer (Garden City, N.Y.: Doubleday Anchor, 1959).

15. Cf. Sören Kierkegaard, *Attack Upon Christendom* (Boston: Beacon Press, 1959); *Sickness Unto Death* (Garden City, N.Y.: Doubleday Anchor, 1954); *The Journals of Kierkegaard*, tr. Alexander Dru (New York: Harper Torchbooks, 1959).

16. Adolf Harnack, *What Is Christianity?* (New York: Harper Torchbooks, 1957), p. 8.

17. *Ibid.*, p. 68.

18. *Ibid.*, p. 275.

19. Walter Rauschenbusch, *A Theology for the Social Gospel* (New York: The Abingdon Press, 1961), p. 49.

20. Karl Barth, *The Word of God and the Word of Man,* tr. Douglas Horton (New York: Harper Torchbooks, 1957), p. 22.

21. *Ibid.,* p. 74.

22. Reinhold Niebuhr, *Moral Man and Immoral Society* (New York: Scribner, 1941), p. xi.

23. Rudolf Bultmann, *Jesus Christ and Mythology* (New York: Scribner, 1958), pp. 35 ff.

24. *Ibid.,* pp. 40–41.

25. *Ibid.,* pp. 84–85. Cf. *Existence and Faith,* tr. Schubert M. Ogden (New York: Living Age Books, 1960).

26. Paul Tillich, *The Dynamics of Faith* (New York: Harper Torchbooks, 1958), p. 46.

27. Paul Tillich, *The Shaking of the Foundations* (New York, Scribner, 1948), p. 57.

28. Paul Tillich, *The Protestant Era,* chapter xi, cited in Robert McAfee Brown, *The Spirit of Protestantism* (New York: Oxford University Press, 1961), p. 43. Cf. also *Dynamics,* p. 29, and John Dillenberger and Claude Welch, *Protestant Christianity* (New York, Scribner, 1954), pp. 313 ff.

29. Louis Bouyer, *The Spirit and Forms of Protestantism,* tr. A. V. Littledale (Westminster, Md.; Newman, 1956), pp. 223–224.

30. Karl Barth, *Evangelical Theology: An Introduction* (New York: Holt, Rinehart, and Winston, 1963), p. 10.

31. Karl Barth, *The Humanity of God* (Richmond, Va.: John Knox Press, 1960), p. 45.

32. *Ibid.,* p. 50.

33. *Ibid.,* p. 80.

34. Emil Brunner, *The Divine Imperative,* tr. O. Wyon (Philadelphia: The Westminster Press, 1957), p. 54.

35. *Ibid.,* p. 119.

36. From *Revelation and Reason,* by Emil Brunner, translated by Olive Wyon. The Westminster Press. Copyright 1946, by W. L. Jenkins. Used by permission.

37. Cf. Aristotle, *Ethics,* VI, 1141a20; *Ethics,* I; *Politics,* I.

38. Emil Brunner, *Revelation and Reason,* p. 349. Cf. Charles N. R.

McCoy, *The Structure of Political Thought* (New York: McGraw-Hill, 1963).

39. Marx, "Economic and Philosophical Manuscripts" in Fromm, *op. cit.*, p. 189.

40. *Ibid.*, p. 132.

41. *Ibid.*, p. 130.

42. *Ibid.*, p. 100; cf. Feuerbach, *The Essence of Christianity*, p. 2.

43. Friedrich Nietzsche, *The Portable Nietzsche*, ed. Walter Kaufmann (New York: Viking, 1954), "Thus Spoke Zarathustra," I, p. 169.

44. "The Gay Science," V, in *ibid.*, p. 447.

45. "Thus Spoke Zarathustra," II, in *ibid.*, p. 198; cf. "The Antichrist," No. 54, in *ibid.*, pp. 636–639.

46. Jean-Paul Sartre, *Existentialism and Human Emotions* (New York: Philosophical Library, 1957), "Existentialism," p. 18.

47. "Existentialism," in *ibid.*, p. 15.

48. "Being and Nothingness," in *ibid.*, p. 63. Cf. Albert Dondeyne, "Problem Raised by Existential Atheism," *Philosophy Today*, Spring 1958, pp. 53–57; Jean Lacroix, "The Meaning and Value of Atheism Today," *Cross Currents*, Summer 1955, pp. 205–219; Jacques Maritain, "On the Meaning of Contemporary Atheism," *Review of Politics*, July 1949, pp. 267–280; C. Fabro, "Le Fondement théorique de l'Atheisme Contemporain," *Sciences Ecclésiastiques*, October–December 1962, pp. 351–374.

49. Christopher Dawson, *America and the Secularization of Modern Culture* (Houston, Texas: University of St. Thomas, 1960), p. 10.

50. It is precisely the violence of the extremes in Protestant attitudes towards God over the centuries that indicated its special problem with the world.

51. Dietrich Bonhoeffer, *Letters and Papers from Prison* (New York: Macmillan, 1962), pp. 164, 218.

52. Thomas J. J. Altizer, "Nirvana and the Kingdom of God," *The Journal of Religion*, April 1963, p. 106. Reprinted by permission of The University of Chicago Press, publishers.

53. *Ibid.*, p. 112.

54. Harvey Cox, *The Secular City* (New York: Macmillan, 1965), p. 6.

55. *Ibid.*, p. 35.

56. Cf. Joshua Lederberg, "Experimental Genetics and Human Evolution," *Bulletin of the Atomic Scientists*, October 1966, pp. 4–10.

57. Gabriel Vahanian, *The Death of God* (New York: George Braziller, 1961), p. 182.

58. Cf. the famous theses of Max Weber, *The Spirit of Capitalism*, and R. H. Tawney, *Religion and the Rise of Capitalism*.

59. E. L. Mascall, *The Secularization of Christianity*, p. 44.

60. Cf. Gabriel Marcel, *The Mystery of Being* (Chicago: Gateway, 1949), Vol. I.

61. Altizer, *op. cit.*, p. 106.

62. Cf. Karl Heim, *Christian Faith and Natural Science* (New York: Harper Torchbooks, 1953).

63. Robert Bruce McLaren, "Science and Contemporary Theology," *Bulletin of the Atomic Scientists*, March 1966, p. 25.

64. Cf. McCoy, *op. cit.*, chapter ii.

65. Cf. Quentin Lauer, "The Genius of Biblical Thought," *The Bridge*, II, 1956–1957, pp. 191–211.

66. Bonhoeffer, *op. cit.*, pp. 194–195.

67. Cf. Aristotle, *Ethics*, VI, 1141a20; *Metaphysics*, I, 982b28. Cf. McCoy, *op. cit.*, chapter iv.

68. Brunner, *Revelation and Reason*, p. 350.

6

The Confrontation with Earthly Realities: All Things Work to the Good

The function and meaning of man, then, is in the world. It is the working out of the purpose of God in the cosmos, it is the love and service of one another. "The faithful, therefore, must learn," as the Council said, "the deepest meaning and the value of all creation, and how to relate it to the praise of God."[1] Yet what is it fundamentally that really makes the Christian world-conscious? What is it that provides the ultimate certitude that God is in truth concerned with the humanity he has created? This ultimate confidence in God is rooted in the Incarnation. Here lies the deepest and most sure pledge of God to man. What, then, does the Incarnation mean to man in the world?

Jesus Christ was born once into this world. He was born in the fullness of time. He was born a child. He was born in a known place, Bethlehem, accepted as the son of a known man, Joseph, a carpenter. He came into the world in this particular way because of the free choice of a finite human person, his mother, Mary. He belonged to the race of Adam, he was a man. He belonged to the House of David, he was a Jew. He was the only Son of the Father. He was in the beginning Word, God.

Such is the Christian belief in the Incarnation. Paradoxically, the Incarnation itself is the one religious and theoretical position that makes it possible to accept simultaneously man's spiritual nature and destiny and his natural material condition and mission as an ordered unity and whole. If man is divided against himself, as it seems evident that he is, it is not primarily because of his essential constitution—that is, a material body and a spiritual soul—but rather because of the choices which he as a person, body and soul acting together, makes. When the Word became flesh man learned the whole dignity of what he was. The Incarnation teaches that the Son of God actually belongs to this world; therefore, his deeds, his choices, are significant beyond passing appearances. The Incarnation is, then, the foundation of that Christian doctrine set forth in Matthew, John, Paul, and James—indeed in the whole of the New Testament—which insists that effective praise and service of the Father must embrace and be manifested in effective and sincere love of one's actual neighbor—a conclusion to which the realities of the world also lead us.

We can, perhaps, appreciate more fully the meaning of this central Christian truth if we refer again to the phenomenon of modern atheism. Atheism and Christianity agree, as we have seen, on one fundamental point. They both insist on the importance of the world itself. Surprisingly, in this respect, a positive and consistent atheism, of all the religions and philosophies available, is closer to Christianity than perhaps any other doctrine. A major reason for this, of course, is that modern atheism, after the seventeenth century, was often in its essence merely Christianity minus the recognition of the supernatural, without the acknowledgment that only God could be God. A deeper reason, however, lies in the rigorously incarnational nature of Christianity, which forces it to accept, almost in spite of itself and its own spiritual temptations (which we have seen to some extent in our discussion of Protestantism), the human and physical world, with all its idiosyncrasies and exigences, as real and good.

Ironically, the surest way to find oneself outside the Christian faith is to deny not the reality of God but the reality of the world. For if we admit the existence of the world but deny the existence of God, there is still hope, the avenue to God is still open. The universe is "word-oriented"; it is God's handiwork, intelligible to the mind of man. But if we deny the reality of the world itself or any of its phenomena— matter, pain, death, goodness or sin—there is no hope. God is dead in that case because man is, quite literally, senseless, without any contact with the world he lives in, and therefore cut off from God, who did come into this world. Strangely enough, it is sometimes harder to believe in the world than in God.

From this point of view, a fairly solid case can be made for the proposition that the most damaging and serious onslaughts against Christianity have originated, not from materialism and worldliness as such, but rather from doctrines and ideas which exalt the spirit at the expense of matter, at the expense of the Incarnation. The abiding doubt in the heart of every Christian centers on the difficulty of accepting the world as it is, a world full of ignorance, sin, and suffering, yet a world

redeemed, a world which God loves. Conversely, the perennial problem of the non-Christian, especially the nonbeliever,
is the fear that this ability of the Christian to confront sin,
weakness, and death involves a rejection of any need for
world improvement. The Christian of today thus finds himself in the highly ambiguous position of striving to uphold two
seemingly contradictory tenets—a belief that death and weakness are inevitable along with an affirmation that the world
can be improved and is *worth* improving.

Actually, there seems to be a problem of considerable depth
here especially for the modern male. A significant body of research and thought has been devoted to the psychological and
spiritual status of the male in modern society. There is a well-
founded suspicion that there is much *angst* among our men.
Clearly men are alienated; they die earlier; they are unsatis-
fied with their world and work. Most corporations have serious leadership problems, as do armies, states, churches, and
schools.

A peculiarly "male" problem exists because men in particular have a haunting doubt about the worth of the world and
its great issues. The female of our race is not so directly exposed to such anguish, since she finds her glory and destiny
more especially in persons, in their lives and uniquenesses. As
yet there does not appear to be any great disorientation among
women, except as a reflection of the male problem, in so far
as woman is directly affected by man's doubts and in so far
as she too must be concerned with the reality outside her
private life.

The male of the race, however, is primarily responsible for

the life in the city, for peace and order, for abundance and scarcity, for culture and art, for science and technology, and the affairs of state. Whenever we find a widespread questioning and disavowal of responsibility for this public task, we can be certain that the male of our species is seriously ill-at-ease with himself and his calling, that things are not well in Zion.

In investigating the cause of such unrest, several explanations are possible. Many are inclined to think that the threat of the bomb and of material obliteration places a more serious strain than we suppose on our psychological structures. Work and confidence in the future depend upon a certain normality and the assurance of a tomorrow, on the belief that one will have a posterity. Scientific progress presupposes order and stability. But present-day man cannot be guaranteed tomorrow.

Modern man has "made his own world." He has approached the destiny Karl Marx sought for him. But he has also created the ways and means and motives to destroy this world of his. Therefore, as the noted anthropologist Margaret Mead has said, "without a future for anyone, anywhere, human life loses its meaning. There is no rationale for the simplest act, no reason to save or to plant or to build. . . . As men see it, this new possibility of total destruction is not an act of God's vengeance . . . but an act that is the outcome of man's fullest development as man."[2]

To reach our fullest development as man, then, seems in the end to mean destroying ourselves and our fellow men. Such is the dilemma. There is much validity in the view that this "threat of war" can be assigned as a cause for the retirement of contemporary man from the world to his own private life. The phenomenon has something Epicurean about it, in the classic sense. Nevertheless one questions whether this explanation gets at the core of the problem. Obviously, if the world is to be destroyed the day after next, there is not much sense in planting a redwood, or even a tulip or a rosebush. But does not modern man's malaise come from a deeper source? Even if the bomb will not be dropped—as we must suppose—still, is he not asking, why plan the garden or renew the city?

Another popular explanation centers on the population explosion: there are going to be too many of us. The most extreme expressions of this view maintain that there is a greater and more certain threat here than in war or the bomb. Since economic and technical developments are self-defeating in the context of rapid population growth, if not actually contributory to it, then why bother? Again, there is here one of the truly serious issues of our era. Political leaders, especially in underdeveloped areas, can be tempted to despair when they see small, hard-fought gains apparently blotted out by greater population increases.

Still another analysis maintains that modern man really has no obvious stake in the world. It is a huge, impersonal mechanism with replaceable parts of which he is one—often one of the more expendable. The Death of a Salesman becomes the fate of everyman. With no real contribution to make, then, man reverts to his private life—if he is rich, to his tinkering, his wine, his dissipation. Even his little growth in knowledge is classed as entertainment, not as culture. If he is poor, he must rely on government doles, on the surplus of an abundant economy, on the psychological fulfillment that comes from television and films.

Nevertheless, all these theories miss the essential issue. Indeed, problems of military warfare, population growth, economic development, and automation have been responsible for the most critical and refined public thinking of our generation. Men concerned seriously about these issues seem to display little of the weakness and lack of balance described by playwrights and novelists depicting the modern man. And if this is correct, then we are back to the problem of atheism and Christianity, to the Incarnation, to the problem of the worthwhileness of the world. And too, we are back to the masculine problem, to the problem of what it is to be a man. For to be a man is to choose, to take responsibility for some real person, some real group, some real institution, some real task in the world. It is to be associated with other men for the common temporal tasks before them. It is to be absolutely realistic about the seriousness of the world, yet with hope and confidence in the knowledge that the world in itself is worth all the effort.

The root of all masculine despair and dejection, consequently, seems to be buried in a doubt, not about one's family and private life, but about the meaning of the eight crucial hours—or whatever it may be—of work that a man must accomplish every day to create the world as he sees it and thereby to establish his dignity as man by helping in this common effort as a legitimate participator. In other words, we have here a doubt about the world itself and its tasks. It is not a question of whether men are going to perform these tasks;

they will be done in some fashion. Rather it is whether these tasks have cosmic meaning at the same time as they are daily, often routine, enterprises in the world.

Thus the prospect of death itself does not seem to be the deepest *angst* for modern man. Rather it is a death which sums up and defines a life that has no abiding, eternal relevance for what it has accomplished during its four score years and ten. The death of a salesman will always be a moving and disturbing experience, even should the salesman be a saint. Yet for our contemporaries the main concern is precisely whether being a salesman for thirty years has any relationship to the significance of his death and its definition of who he is, and, further, whether his life's work really does benefit his fellow man.

The issue between the atheist and the Christian, consequently, is not the profound significance of the world and work in it—they agree in this—but the relevance of the world and its work to the persons with whom one is more or less permanently associated and to the greater community of persons which defines ultimate reality itself. Oriental religions and some forms of Western asceticism have often, and plausibly, argued that man's experience of pleasure, honors, and service to the state will, if seen honestly, clearly reveal the ephemeral nature of these goals and thus of the world. The inevitable conclusion seemed to be, Why, then, worry about them? They cannot yield God. If that is so, atheism has logically retorted, then obviously we must reject God. For if all these things become a matter of indifference because God is not found in them, then God is man's enemy: the world is something man simply must not ignore.

THE EARTHLY TASK

Christianity, however, has read the New Testament. God became man. The Word, in whom all things are created, became flesh. The power of God given to man is itself creative. Man's task is not just to receive life, but to give it to others once he has received it. He is to subdue the earth, to multiply, to go forth and teach all nations. As we have repeatedly emphasized, God is so great that he can give creatures the power to act for themselves *freely*. Indeed, the whole natural and supernatural effort of man is to realize all things in *freedom*. It is the glory of the order of salvation in which we live that God does nothing significant for man without man's free acceptance of God's initial gift. There is a true sense in which all progress in the world, in the state as well as in the Church, is growth in the recognition of freedom, in the freedom of God as well as in the freedom of man. The Redemption itself, which in its radical postulate is a pure, unmerited gift of God to man, as both Luther and Trent agreed, divinizes man, giving him the active power to complete the task of God in the world, the restoration of all things in Christ. And while this restoration cannot be totally accomplished in this life, what can be done should be done. Man is free to accept or to reject this mission.

There is a true earthly task given to men. They have something they *must* accomplish as men. "Throughout the course of the centuries, men have labored to better the circumstances of their lives through a monumental amount of individual and collective effort. To believers, this point is settled: considered in itself, such human activity accords with God's will."[3] Men are responsible for the generations, for the world, for the full development of the earthly city. This is their dignity. A failure to participate in this task—even if only in the most menial jobs—is self-destructive. Yves Simon used to say that if you paid a man an extremely high salary to dig a hole six-by-six and then to fill it up again immediately and to start over, and if this were his sole job, he would soon go mad. What we are witness to in our own shops and offices, in our plays and novels, in our schools and agencies and churches is, very often, this doubt about man's purpose in the world for which he is responsible. This, it seems, is the spiritual problem of our times.[4]

Many Christians are opposed to any cosmic conception of Christ. In one sense, certainly, these theologians are merely trying to oppose oversimplification, to avoid the view that keeps cropping up in all religions—namely, that the order on earth should be an exact image of the order in the physical heavens. Sometimes, however, the implication is that the vastness of the universe could have nothing to do with Ephesians 1, Colossians 1, or the prologue to John. Yet this is exactly where we must take our stand. We must really believe that God is great enough to have created precisely *this* universe, that the Word became flesh in *this* world, that all things return through man, through Christ to the Father, that therefore what man does has cosmic significance since the world is for man. The cosmos and Christianity, as we have seen earlier, do belong together.

Many will object that it is arrogance and stupidity to make man the center of the universe. Nevertheless, to repeat what we have already argued, it is man who knows, whose mind seeks quite literally to know all things, whose corporate effort more and more illumines the places in which we dwell. Further, it is not man who makes himself the key creature that he is. It is God in the Incarnation who does so. Man is the masterwork of creation because the Word became man. The destiny of man in the world is to humanize it, to spiritualize it. All things return to the Father through man. Man returns to God through the Son and the Spirit.

The core of the personal life of God is, as we recall, societal. In giving man a true task to accomplish in the universe, in further divinizing him so that he shares this trinitarian life, God has complimented man by leaving to him the mission of bringing material creation into the service of human persons through the use of his mind and hands. This is the common effort in which all men are engaged. Material creation must be brought by man into the service of persons. The whole Christian theology of the sacraments is here involved. For the sacraments are God's way of using the world and human nature, signs and symbols, in his personal communion with man. The sacraments are the here-and-now continuation of the Incarnation in the world, the here-and-now continuation of the communion of God and man. Even in the supernatural order, God has respected man's relationship to the material world. In this way, he has again looked upon creation and seen that it is very good.

But persons are *for* one another, as they are in the Trinity; they are society, they are to be one, they are to be forever. The life of God is *agape*, eternal life. The end of man is *agape*, eternal life. Men's common goal in material creation is the society of persons, the *koinonia*, the fellowship. This is why all true manhood must be both earthly-oriented—the earth must be transformed—and person-oriented—the actual neighbor must be loved while on earth. Man is, in the end, *for* man. This is the eternal decree by which he is also *for* God, and *for* the world. If we are witnessing in our day a crisis of manhood, it is because men in their actual lives entertain a doubt about the meaning of the world and of persons. This doubt cuts them off from the world itself, and therefore from the possibility of true love and true redemption, since it was to this imperfect, changing, plastic world that Christ came and which he transformed. Ultimately, we cannot be men and doubt the world. Man must choose and commit himself to what exists, to the world and to persons in it.

In these times, we cannot but be astonished by the immediacy with which the sufferings and anguish of our fellow men break in upon our consciousness. The litany of this generation's disasters, trials and wrongs is a long one— poverty, wars, overpopulation, self-willed leaders, persecution, intolerance. Yet on all sides, all our public and private institutions, all our leaders cry out that these issues are for us to confront—that they represent our vocation to the world.

The Incarnation has, so to speak, divinized this vocation of man to his world. It was Tertullian who remarked in a beautiful phrase that the "hinge of salvation is the flesh." This must mean not just that Christ became man, that the principle of our eternal life was present amongst us, but also that on whatever the flesh suffers, whatever it experiences—its joys, triumphs, defeats, pains, and sins—salvation hinges. For these are exactly the pressing realities which God has left it to human freedom to transform in grace. We have a spiritual problem, we have a painful emptiness in our hearts, because we do not as men and as societies take seriously enough this call given to us both by God and by our fellow man.

"But to all who did accept him he gave the power to become children of God." (John 1:12) To "accept" *him* is to accept all flesh, for this is what he took on in the Incarnation. The Incarnation is the divine sign of our vocation to the whole physical and spiritual world, to the whole world of man. When we think of the Incarnation, when we celebrate it in its great feast, this is what we rejoice in: the union of the divine nature with the nature of man; the warmth and love we have for one another because, with Christ present among us as a child, we have certainty that our human enterprises and efforts are meaningful, worthwhile.

GOD'S ABSOLUTE RESPECT FOR HUMAN CHOICE

To believe in God would presumably be much more simple if the world were not faced with such disturbing problems as sin, suffering, evil, death, and finiteness. If we are going to confront the earthly realities, we must soon see that these too turn on the hinge that is the flesh. In the face of these darker human issues, Christianity occupies a special place among the theologies and philosophies of this world because of its belief that the God-man shared in the consequences of our human condition. In a real sense, because of the Incarnation, man cannot use the evils of the world as the basis of a revolt against God. Indeed the doctrine of original sin means precisely that man, not God, is the fundamental cause of sin and suffering in this particular world in which we are. These are, perhaps, harsh sayings. Nevertheless the Christian vision of God inviting man to share his trinitarian life has as its focal point the Cross, the place where the God-man died. For the Christian, it is not possible to believe that the consequences of sin and evil have not been seen in their fullness by God, because the Son of God, the second person in the Trinity, himself experienced them. To be a Christian, therefore, means to keep faith in God in the midst of the darkness of our life on earth.

If we are to grasp the true import of the Christian doctrines of evil, sin, death, suffering, and hell, we must begin by seeing that they all make man and his world *more* important, not less. It is customary in polemics to base doubts about the possibility of God's existence upon the existence of imperfection and evil in the world.[5] The time-worn argument is that a God who was all-good could not allow innocent suffering, could not tolerate the existence of malice, could not condemn anyone to hell forever. Indeed, such arguments are not merely a matter of polemics, no human being sincere with himself can avoid their force. But what is of special interest in such objections is that they all implicitly deny, or tend to deny, the possibility of freedom in the creature. A denial of freedom by itself, of course, does not remove these realities from the scene; it merely renders them almost completely unintelligible. The doctrines of sin, evil, death, and suffering, evidence the serious significance with which God has endowed man. Indeed, more than this, they are evidence of the reality of love in the finite world. For the possibility of love is the possibility of meaningful choice, of real alternatives. Even God must risk that men will not choose him; he must risk this if he really wishes to be loved.

God respects his creation. This means that the possibility of choosing against God must exist. That is to say, were God to insist on redressing immediately and by force every evil and sin in the world the minute it occurred, there would be no real freedom to choose against God. The significance of this is often missed. It means that the history of mankind is a working out of the choice of mankind for good and evil. It means further that when man chooses to harm his neighbor, his neighbor, even if perfectly innocent, will be harmed. God will not interfere.[6] On the other hand, all good as well as all evil takes place in a social context. The act that harms the innocent becomes the cause for a counter-act to protect the innocent, to repair the damage. It becomes the cause of repentance.[7] All this means that the consequences of good and evil actions take their course. When God allows for man, he allows for the whole sequence of the results of man's actions. Man is free to affect his neighbors, both in space and in time— those who live beside him, those who come after him. The world is not merely a stage in which all things happen mechanically according to the script. It is rather for man in his personal and social history to see that his love, his sense of responsibility, shall become the guiding spirit of his life and his society.

Man chooses this course, he cannot be forced to it. To rebel against God because he does not immediately prevent the evil of man's actions is to degrade man, not to exalt him. For, as we have said, it is merely another way of refusing to admit

that God could create a free creature, that a free creature
really has an absolute area of responsibility, an absolute power
of choice. Ultimately, this is what man is always tempted to
deny, that the responsibility is his own. The last word on
this is that of Paul: "It was not for any fault on the part of
creation that it was made unable to attain its purpose, it was
made so by God. . . . We know that by turning everything
to their good God co-operates with all those who love him,
with all those that he has called according to his purpose."
(Romans 8:20, 28)

THE DOCTRINE OF HELL: MAN IS ALONE

The skeptic argues impressively that a God who invented
hell could hardly be a good God, or if he were good, an all-
powerful one. But the question involved here is rather one of
theological fact—who in fact did "invent" hell? Christian
doctrine holds clearly that hell is man's invention, not God's.[8]
Naturally, at first sight this seems to beg the question. For,
according to Christians, God created man; therefore, if he
knew man could choose hell—as he must be presumed to have
known—his responsibility for the existence of hell remains.
Perhaps we shall never fully settle this agonizing question, but
we can get some light on it if we remove a few grave mis-
understandings. The problem is always wrongly stated when
God is conceived as some sort of high monarch arbitrarily
casting a struggling, helpless subject onto an eternal gridiron,
as classical imagery seems to suggest. Different generations
use different images to depict hell. We must not let our
images obscure the doctrine.[9] The essential point about hell

is that God respects absolutely man's truly free choice. This is really what the argument is about. We can describe the result of this choice in terms of God's rejection of man to make graphic the point about the absolute separation involved. But hell is not God's rejection of man; it is man's refusal of God's invitation, man's choice to be alone, by himself, forever; to be, if he can, the ultimate cause of his own world.

Now we can perhaps in theory ask the question, Why does not God force man to choose him? The question, however, comes down to a more disturbing difficulty. For if man were forced to love God, this would mean the removal of hell as a possibility. And this would mean the removal of man as man, for it would imply that God could not really create a free creature. But we want man to be man. In other words, the rejection of the belief in hell always seems to diminish the power of God, and more especially to diminish the dignity of man. Thus what seems to be, at first sight, most objectionable in the Christian vision really turns out to be connected with the very basis of the dignity of man in the world.

In calling forth the free creature, then, God gave man the possibility of choosing something worthwhile; indeed, he gave him the possibility of choosing an incredible variety of worthwhile things. What makes the choice of something other than God result in hell is not the worthwhileness of man's task in the world or the value of the things themselves, but the isolation of these things from the whole, the erecting of them into a mere instrument of the self. What really results in hell, therefore, is the final choice of the self as the highest thing in one's world, the refusal to open oneself to the gift of another person. This is destructive of the person's relation with God because, as we have suggested, person in God is, of its very structure, open to other persons. To be a person is to be open to the gift of another. When a person refuses this openness, this gift of another, he condemns himself to be what a person cannot be, namely, alone.

Thus, when such a choice of the self is really and absolutely made by a truly free creature—we do not know for certain whether anyone has ever actually made this final choice— it is respected by God. Man is left alone forever. This is what he has chosen. He does not will to change, this is what his will demands. Nothing can change this. Hell, then, does not show how small man is in the eyes of God. Just the opposite. Hell is, paradoxically, the belief that the free creature is the most important thing in creation, that the consequences of his actions are in fact eternal. This is why it is of such profound importance that we do love one another, that we do see the significance of our life together, that we do help one another. There is an alternative to living the life of the triune God to which he has invited us. There is the alternative of living one's eternal life alone.

The choice to live alone forever is just that, a choice. Some like to argue that this life is not long enough to make such a choice, that man is too weak for such a burden. Perhaps it is true, four score and ten years may not be enough. Maybe two centuries of life on earth or even three would suffice. In this hypothesis, if man chooses hell the first time around, then he should be given a second or third turn to change his mind. Yet merely to state such viewpoints serves to illustrate that they really demean the man who actually does exist. The choice of man takes place in a lifetime, in a history whereby a person experiences the life God gives him, the realities of childhood, adolescence, marriage, sickness, social life, parenthood, work, old age, and death. In any lifetime, a man is sufficiently exposed to other persons, to the world, for him to make up his mind actually how he will stand in relation to others. In this context, no matter how small it appears on the scene of history, the life of a man on earth will reveal his willingness to be for or against others who have come across the path of his own concrete life in the world. And our relations with other persons always involve our relation to the world in which we live. Indeed, the world is essential if we are to aid or to reject our neighbor. It is the arena of his human actions. "Lord, when did we see you hungry and feed you; or thirsty and give you drink? When did we see you a stranger and make you welcome; naked and clothe you; sick or in prison and go to see you?" (Matthew 25:38–39) This choice takes place among the least of the brethren as well as among the greatest. This means that we have a final choice to make with our freedom, an ultimate choice which structures our life on earth. We always have enough time to make this choice, a lifetime. " 'Ah, no, father Abraham,' said the rich man, 'but if someone comes to them from the dead, they will repent.' Then Abraham said to him, 'If they will not listen either to Moses or to the prophets, they will not be convinced even if someone should rise from the dead.' " (Luke 16:31) There is, then, no point in extending the suspense of this final choice to two or three or four lifetimes. There is no profit in sending the dead back to warn us. These things would make no difference. A human life, therefore, is of absolute importance to God because it is the risk God took in creation, the risk of allowing man to choose his destiny.

THE REDEMPTION FROM SIN

Hell represents God's choice to allow man his own world. On man's part, hell is chosen in sin. The doctrine of sin underscores the importance of each single human action. Each action made sinful has eternal consequences, as does each action of man's concern and kindness.[10] But the sin that results in hell is only the sin or the life of sin that is final, that orientation away from God which the person accepts at death as wholly his own. That hell is not the inevitable consequence of sin is due to the mercy of God, to the present order of salvation in which man is allowed to repent.[11]

We shall recall from our discussion of original sin earlier in this book that God's initial intention to associate free beings with himself in his eternal life carried with it the possibility that some creatures would reject the world mission and destiny offered to them. Hence man's rejection was above all an abuse of his liberty: "Although he was made by God in a state of holiness, from the very dawn of history man abused his liberty, at the urging of personified Evil. Man set himself against God and sought to find fulfillment apart from God."[12] What man chose, God respected. Original sin, therefore, means essentially that man chose a wrong orientation towards God. God accepted the orientation which man had chosen.

However, man was still free. Hence when God responded to man's need in the incarnation of the God-man, in the initiation of the sacramental order of salvation, it meant that he would use man's chosen condition as a way to lead him back to the divine purpose: to share God's eternal life. "Now before we came of age we were as good as slaves to the elemental principles of this world, but when the appointed time came, God sent his Son, born of a woman, born a subject of the Law, to redeem the subjects of the Law and to enable us to be adopted as sons. The proof that you are sons is that God has sent the Spirit of his Son into our hearts: the Spirit that cries, 'Abba, Father,' and it is this that makes you a son. . . ." (Galatians 4:3–7) In other words, even the sins of man could be forgiven, could become in their results, as we so easily recall from the case of the Magdalene, the means of leading men back to God. Man was no longer helpless before his sins and their consequences; they too were redeemed, because all things work to the good in God's providence. This is the crux of the Redemption, for which we found the longing so real in our survey of modern literature.

Sin is not an easy thing to understand. Indeed, almost the only way to acquire any adequate notion of sin and its meaning is through Scripture, for the depth of sin is the depth of the concern of God for his creation. The question of human sin, the turning away from God through one's neglect or harm of someone God has created, requires that we consider how it is possible that sin can be forgiven, can fit into God's overall purpose in creation. Sin could be forgiven: this was the claim of the God-man. "And at this some scribes said to themselves, 'This man is blaspheming.' Knowing what was in their minds Jesus said, 'Why do you have such wicked thoughts in your hearts? Now, which of these is easier: to say, "Your sins are forgiven," or to say, "Get up and walk"?' "

(Matthew 9:3–5) This power was left to his followers in
the sacramental order. Sacraments are signs, visible symbols,
actions performed within the Church for the individual man
who is to be saved. Sacraments bring the total redemptive
effort of the risen Christ to bear on a particular person.
Sacraments are God's initiative, God's call, since all steps to
salvation must begin with God.[13] What Christ did on earth,
his dying and rising again for all men, must actually touch
the redeemed person.

Christ is the visible sign of God in the world, he is "God's
way of being a man." Christ is the manner in which God
respects man, he is the divine acceptance of man's corporeality
as real and as significant. "In his body lives the fullness of
divinity, and in him you too find your fulfillment. . . ."
(Colossians 2:9) Christ is the assurance on the part of God
that he will deal with man in a human, personal, tangible
way. "Verbum in carne caro, ita homo in Deo Deus est" is
Vincent of Lérins' concise way of summing up this principle.[14]

SIN AND ITS FORGIVENESS

The origin of sin is always pictured in Scripture as man's
act, his free choice. Yet, as we have pointed out, God's reaction in the face of this fact is not to remove freedom in order
to make man's beatitude a certainty. In one sense man's freedom has been a mixed blessing for him: somehow it is always
associated with the reality of sin. Consequently the mission
of Christ in the world is to redeem the power of freedom,
even though it may still be employed against God. This redemption of freedom involved two steps. The first was the

removal of what might be called, in the language of the book of Revelation (20:15), the "first death," Adam's blighted legacy. This was accomplished for the race by Christ on the Cross. The true descendants of Abraham now live by faith in Christ Jesus. (Cf. Romans 4:16; Galatians 3:1–14.) The Cross and the Resurrection reestablished the avenue to eternal life with God; his initial intention could again be accomplished. Christ, therefore, redeemed all sin: "It is all God's work. It was God who reconciled us to himself through Christ and gave us the work of handing on this reconciliation. In other words, God in Christ was reconciling the world to himself, not holding men's faults against them, and he has entrusted to us the news that they are reconciled." (2 Corinthians 5:19; cf. 1 Timothy 4:10)

Nevertheless, as Paul noted again and again, the mystery of iniquity remained among Christians. (2 Thessalonians 2:7) Baptism is the initial rebirth by which Christ's act of redemption is conferred on man, incorporating him into Christ. (Colossians 2:12; Romans 6:3 ff.) But there is also need for penance, by which the Apostles were given power through the Holy Spirit to remit sins. (John 20:22 ff.) This is the redemption of liberty which involved both the power to forgive the personal sins of men and the power to restore man to the Father's favor in faith and baptism. The mystery of iniquity, which is at the root of man's personal sins, tainting his freedom, must be overcome by man in Christ through forgiveness.

For Paul, sin consisted in many things, as the long lists of specific disorders noted in Romans, Corinthians, Colossians, and most of the other Epistles suggest. The miracles of Christ were almost always not only a sign of Christ's divinity but also a reminder of the reality of sin. The prophets had constantly pointed out the sincere sorrow for sin required in one who turned to God. Christ's miracles always contained an implicit challenge to man's security: If this is God, we must turn and be converted to his ways. Yet all these miracles could be rejected, the sign from God could be ignored. "Then, grieved to find them so obstinate, he looked angrily round at them, and said to the man, 'Stretch out your hand.' He stretched it out and his hand was better. The Pharisees went out and at once began to plot with the Herodians against him, discussing how to destroy him." (Mark 3:5–6)

The very existence of sin in the New Testament demands its ultimate resolution. There are two parallel themes with regard to the future time of expectation before God reestablishes all things. First is the theme of sin itself, the sin of the species and the sins of individuals. God's will is ultimately to destroy these sins; if they are not forgiven, the sinners are to be withdrawn eternally from the life of God, as the discussion on hell has brought out. But Christ's mission was forgiveness, not punishment. "My brothers, I want you to realize that it is through him that forgiveness of your sins is proclaimed. Through him justification from all sins which the Law of Moses was unable to justify is offered to every believer." (Acts 13:38–39; cf. 1 Thessalonians 5:8–11.) "The next day, seeing Jesus coming towards him, John said, 'Look, there is the lamb of God that takes away the sin of the world.'" (John 1:29) It is always hoped that man will freely choose to acknowledge his sin. In all of this, God always respects his creation. Freedom will not be removed. "When

Christ freed us, he meant us to remain free." (Galatians 5:1)

The second theme is the restoration of all things on earth and in heaven, the transformation of the earth by man in charity. (Colossians 3:10 ff.; Ephesians 1:3–23) This is a plan "he so kindly made in Christ from the beginning to act upon when the times had run their course to the end; that he would bring everything together under Christ, as head, everything in the heavens and everything on earth." (Ephesians 1:9–10) These notions of sin and restoration converge. By his prayers and penance man can actually be said to hasten the Second Coming. (2 Thessalonians 2:1 ff.; 3:1 ff.; 2 Peter 3:12) Therefore the completion of man's total presence with Christ before the Father, which was God's intention in creating man, is dependent upon his repentance. The "increase, multiply, and subdue the earth" command of Genesis is a necessary mission of man on earth, a mission which is hindered by sin. All things must be redeemed, even the effects of sin, as Augustine long ago suggested. The mission of man is to transform not merely the physical world but the moral world as well. (Cf. Colossians 3:8–10.) The transformation, the spiritualization, of the physical world is clearly effected by the labor of the mind and heart in charity. Its ultimate meaning is that "when everything is subjected to him, then the Son himself will be subject in his turn to the One who subjected all things to him, so that God may be all in all." (1 Corinthians 15:28)

SIN AND LOVE

The question still remains, What about sins? "How will I ever forgive myself for all the things I've done?"—this is the abiding question Styron asked in *Set This House on Fire,* as we have seen.[15] The primary sin in the New Testament is the failure to love our neighbor as Christ has loved him. Translated into terms of world transformation, the primary sin is the failure to use the goods and talents God has given to us for our neighbor. (Matthew 25:44 ff.) What of personal sins, all of which are, as Aquinas taught, violations of charity in their ultimate malice?[16] "Here is a saying that you can rely on and nobody should doubt: that Christ Jesus came into the world to save sinners." (1 Timothy 1:15) Sins can be forgiven. This is the constant teaching of the New Testament. The teaching of Christ and Paul, baptism and penance make this abundantly clear. (Cf. Matthew 9:4–6.)

The problem of personal sin, however, is not settled merely with a knowledge that it can be forgiven. Man must first acknowledge and admit the reality of the sin. All sins are violations of love. Whatever the category in which a sin may be specifically classified—murder, lying, robbery, rape, blasphemy—it is sinful because it somehow hurts some person whom God loves. Even the sin of blasphemy, aside from all scandal, hurts primarily the blasphemer, whom God loves.

Clearly, God himself is not hurt by sin. He is always at peace within himself. Nothing in creation can "hurt" God if we use the term strictly. But God has committed himself to creatures through his love. Creatures can refuse this personal self-giving of God by sin and thereby offend his love. Therefore, man must recognize his own act in the hurt and anguish he causes to another. And he must also recognize in this same act the divine presence, because that act wounds some "little one" whom God loves. For this he is responsible. His humanity, his recognition of himself as a creature, depends upon his willingness to make this admission.

It is this sinfulness, this admission of specific acts and attitudes, that man must confess, because these acts are violations of the personal love between himself, God, and other persons. All repentance is the expression of the hatred and detestation of these particular sinful acts, together with a turning from them with regret and sincerity to the salvation offered in Christ Jesus. Even the beginnings of this turning are from God, but they are properly man's personal actions also. Sinful acts, then, can be and are redeemed. "For this reason I tell you that her sins, her many sins, must have been forgiven her, or she would not have shown such great love. It is the man who is forgiven little who shows little love." (Luke 7:47)

EVEN SINS WORK UNTO THE GOOD

A sinful act, rooted in the mystery of iniquity, is a reality set loose in the world. Once launched on its course, it is bound to exert its effect on the world, even granting that it is subsequently repented. Since it is disruptive of order, sin leaves a vacuum, a true absence of the goodness and love which should be present and effective in the world. In this sense, though we cannot demand it, we do depend on one another's love. The lack of this order which should be present makes further disorder possible. The obvious problem is this: Can men really forgive themselves for their sins? Can they face what they failed to do when given an opportunity? Is not the evil that men cause, the suffering and harm to others, simply too vast even to hope that these sinful acts and their consequences can be repaired?

Man cannot forgive his own sins, but God can. This is the New Testament teaching. For this doctrine to be meaningful, however, we still must ask whether the evil caused to the innocent by sin, even the harm caused to the guilty, can really be repaired. To this dilemma, there is only one Christian answer, that of Paul: "We know that by turning everything to their good God co-operates with all those who love him, with all those that he has called according to his purpose." (Romans 8:28) Augustine added to this that "even sin" worked to the good because God can use it too for salvation.

Is this an answer? It is the answer God gives to freedom. To conceive of the impossibility of these crimes of man against man, to maintain that God could not allow them, is, in a way, to deny God's power to make man. And God makes man free. He allows him his evil. But the redemptive order of love is a redemption of man in his weakness and sin. The man whom God loves is not the perfect man who cannot sin, but the weak, changeable man who does sin. The pledge of God in Christ is that sin will not ultimately lead to evil but to good. The divine symbol of this is the Cross.

The *felix culpa* is an operative power in human history. The Old Testament had plainly taught that God could and did use the sins of men for the punishment and reform of Israel. The present sins of men—the sins against children, against minorities, against the poor, against the sick, against the honest, against the just, against the loyal—must be acknowledged in order to be forgiven. Yet these sins too work into God's plan of leading men back to participate in his life. This is the central meaning of the Crucifixion. "Instead of that, he has made his appearance once and for all, now at the end of the last age, to do away with sin by sacrificing himself." (Hebrews 9:26)

These very sins of man, however, are also the ones that militate against man's fulfilling his primary vocation with regard to nature, the transformation of the earth for the welfare of mankind. There is, as we have noted above, an intimate relationship between repentance and the transformation of the earth. Penance is that part of the sacramental order, that part of Christ's personal relationship to men, which deals with men's personal sins. It is the rite through which sins are transformed in faith, according to which they now work unto the good. Man must detest his sin, he must acknowledge it to himself and God before one who listens and absolves in the Church in Christ's name. But sins should not and must not cause despair. This is the abiding lesson taught to us by Judas. Sin can now become salvific and regenerative because we are in Christ. "For our sake God made the sinless one into sin, so that in him we might become the goodness of God." (2 Corinthians 5:21) Sorrow passes into charity, and charity transforms the earth.

The relationship between the "repent and believe" of the primitive kerygma and the cosmic vision of Colossians and Ephesians is, then, very intimate. Penance is the beginning of the transformation of the earth in this life in that it restores men to love of one another and promotes the healing and liberation of mankind—and not only mankind but the whole of nature, which in some mysterious fashion suffered the repercussions of man's fall: "The whole creation is eagerly waiting for God to reveal his sons. It was not for any fault on the part of creation that it was made unable to attain its purpose, it was made so by God; but creation still retains the hope of being freed, like us, from its slavery to decadence, to enjoy the same freedom and glory as the children of God. From the beginning till now the entire creation, as we know, has been groaning in one great act of giving birth; and not only creation, but all of us who possess the first-fruits of the Spirit, we too groan inwardly as we wait for our bodies to be set free." (Romans 8:19–23)

Christians are saved from being cast into despair by their sins through the presence of the risen Christ before the Father, standing to make intercession for us. No sin is so disruptive that the wisdom of God cannot use its consequences for the good. "I am writing this, my children, to stop you sinning; but if anyone should sin, we have our advocate with the Father, Jesus Christ, who is just; he is the sacrifice that takes our sins away, and not only ours, but the whole world's." (1 John 2:1–2) This is the ultimate significance of the function of repentance and penance in the world. The reality of personal sin is touched by Christ in a sacramental way in his Church. By this means, sin is redeemed. It is now ordered back into God's mystery following his providential plan of associating man with himself in this salvific endeavor. Man's repentance thus becomes an essential aspect of the way all things return to the Father, of the way man confronts the earthly realities that surround him.

EVIL AND ACTION

The mystery of evil is not easy for man to come to grips with, and part of the problem is one of definition. Hell, in itself, is evil; yet, as we have suggested, it is good that God respects the choice of the man who chooses to be alone. Suffering is evil, it should not be present in a healthy being; yet it is good that we experience the warning of pain; it is the body's means of letting us know something is wrong. Without pain, we could not live for very long. Sin is evil, yet sin teaches repentance, mercy, and forgiveness.[17] Death is evil, yet it can be a blessing. It is the end of a life that must end.

Nevertheless the presence of evil in the world is a certainty. What should be our attitude towards it? First it is necessary to understand the difference between evil and finiteness. This distinction is important, for human limitations are the major cause of practical human difficulties, not evil itself. The main danger man faces is the temptation to attribute to evil what is really and simply the consequence of finiteness. The rebellion against finiteness on the grounds that it is evil is really the rebellion against the world as it is. If we think our inability to fly like a bird or run like a deer, for example, is the result of evil rather than the limitations imposed by what we are, then our rebellion is directed at the very structure of reality. Man's first problem is always to recognize his own finiteness, his own limitedness.

Finiteness, moverover, indicates the arena in which man can act. The mission to humanize the world is primarily a mission of finiteness; it would have been man's task even without original sin. Man, being a man, would always have to learn as a man, gradually. We have noted that pain is a good whereby we can know that something is wrong with us. That man's struggle to order and control pain in this life has been so long-drawn-out is the consequence of our finiteness. Presumably God could have created man capable of knowing by instinct all the pain-killing devices we now know. But he did not so create man. To conquer pain becomes the task of science, experience, and charity. Pain is something finiteness challenges men to confront.

Evil, on the other hand, implies more than finiteness. There is a kind of evil occurring every day which is not really evil in the sense that blame for it can be assigned. If a man loses his arm because a rock falls on it while he is climbing in the mountains, it is evil for him that his arm is gone. He should have the arm, obviously. Nevertheless, the falling rock was doing exactly what rocks are supposed to do. It is absolutely essential for the world that rocks fall; without gravity there could be no world. This kind of resultant evil that happens to an individual is actually the product of finiteness, our inability to foresee or to stop every danger to the individual.

Real evil is that chosen by men. This is always the context of sin and hell, the context of free choice, the refusal to respect creation and persons. That evil exists in human society in addition to mere finiteness, there is little need to argue. The whole social fabric of mankind is concerned with limiting and controlling the expansion of evil. The tragedy of evil is not merely that men choose to harm their neighbors, but that they fail to place in the world actions that can be positive helps to others for whom they are responsible.

The problem of evil, however, is important in this present context in explaining not so much why it can exist as whether man is completely helpless before it. In discussing hell, we have seen that the possibility of evil is associated with the nature of finite freedom. The social fabric of personal human life at all levels is such that it is "other-oriented." The precise origin of concrete evil as it is experienced in human life is the deliberate rejection of the objective demands of the social order, of this "other-orientation" of personal life. This is true even when one is looking only at oneself, for the gift of oneself to the world is something that is meant for others, something that God has not placed in the world just for our own enjoyment. One of the great problems of man is always how he is to react to evil within society, at whatever level it may be found—personal, family, state, business, international. How and whether to act in the face of evil, indeed, is one of the most crucial problems that man must face.

Man's most instinctive reaction to evil is that he can have nothing to do with it. This reaction is normal enough, yet logically it has its problems. For it can lead to a gradual withdrawal from the world of men where evil is actually found. In other words, when so-called good people decide to be purists, to have nothing to do with evil, to stand back from corrupt society or corrupt individuals, they in effect make possible precisely the opposite state to that which they desire. For they actually multiply evil by leaving the field free to those who have little scruple with the good. Therefore, man cannot simply "withdraw" from the evil world in some simple or naive fashion. For, as we have seen, if one does not admit the possibility of the presence of God and evil in the same universe—which is logically what someone who wants nothing to do with evil really believes—only two alternatives remain. Either God does not exist or evil is something that can be removed by unaided human effort. But if God does not exist, the evil is still there. The problem remains. And we are beginning to see that man can only remove some of the evil and suffering in the world. Thus the second alternative vanishes also. Only despair seems left. Yet despair attacks freedom, and freedom is what establishes man as an autonomous person able to react against evil.

Christian theology has not neglected this area. It has recognized that there are actions which do have evil effects connected with them and still may have to be performed in spite of these effects. Further, it is recognized that forcible, even violent, action taken against evil action is itself good and just. It is true that the conditions for such individual or social reaction to evil have been carefully hedged in with restrictions of intention, means, and proportion; but in the final analysis man has not found himself paralyzed in the face of evil that comes from mankind. In confronting evil, man must always choose the good; or, the lesser evil, when he has no other real alternative. When his action or lack of action results in causing greater evil, man is not free to claim that his responsibility to the good excused him from guilt when he could have prevented the greater evil with the lesser one. Evil will always have its effects, which must be counteracted, but the nature of the human situation in the actual world demands that man confront and limit it with all the vigor at his disposal.

Sin, evil, freedom, finiteness, suffering present man with his most difficult problems in his confrontation with God. None the less, the complex relations man has with God do not allow him to conclude that these harsh realities prove that God is not concerned for his creation. Quite the opposite seems true. For we must weigh evil and hell against the gifts of human freedom and human dignity; suffering and death against the amazing gift of life itself; all the sorrows and sufferings of sinful humanity against the coming of the Redeemer. The order of reality in which we now live is one that seems at first sight to be alienated from God. Behind it, however, stands God's abiding choice to accept man for what he is, to respond to his needs, to respect his choices, even his eternal choices.

If, then, man chooses suffering, God will choose suffering. If man chooses death, God will choose death. If man sins, God will forgive. All this recalls the fundamental point about the inner life of God. It is a life of "otherness," of persons concerned with persons. It is a life into which man in the context of his history is invited. But to accept this invitation, man must choose others, leave himself open to the gifts he has been chosen to receive. Should man refuse to do this, God allows him his own particular choices. He invites others to share his life. The Kingdom of God is social; the man who chooses to be alone chooses against it. Yet, in all else, all things work to the good; even sin, evil, and death finally find their place in the choice of God to invite others to share his inner life. The Incarnation overshadows all these realities of the world. It is God's response to what man has made for himself. It is the constant reminder of how much God has loved his work of creation, the reminder that he loved it, such as it was, to the end. "It was before the festival of the Passover, and Jesus knew that the hour had come for him to pass from this world to the Father. He had always loved those who were his in the world, but now he showed how perfect his love was." (John 13:1)

NOTES

1. "Dogmatic Constitution on the Church," *The Documents of Vatican II*, ed. Walter Abbott, no. 36, p. 62.

2. Margaret Mead, *The Saturday Review of Literature*, June 1, 1963, p. 11.

3. "The Church Today," *The Documents of Vatican II*, ed. Walter Abbott, no. 34, p. 232.

4. Cf. the call of the whole Church to holiness in "The Church Today," *ibid.*, nos. 39–42, pp. 237–242.

5. These are, indeed, the two main objections Aquinas poses to the existence of God. Cf. *Summa Theologica*, I, 2, a. 3.

6. Something of this problem is seen in Alberto Moravia's *The Two Women*, tr. Angus Davidson (New York: Signet).

7. Cf. Thomas Aquinas, *Summa Theologica*, I, 2, 3, ad 1; I–II, 79, 4, ad 1; I–II, 73, 4, ad 3.

8. Cf. Denzinger, nos. 443, 342, 1002, 1306.

9. Cf. Robert W. Gleason, "Hell: An Apology," *Thought*, Summer 1958, pp. 165–182.

10. Cf. Thomas Aquinas, *Summa Theologica*, II–II, 14, 3; *Contra Gentiles*, III, 139.

11. In Aquinas' view this constituted the difference between men and angels, who were able to posit their destiny in one act. Cf. *Contra Gentiles*, 4, 95.

12. "The Church in the Modern World," *The Documents of Vatican II*, ed. Walter Abbott, no. 13, p. 211.

13. Cf. Denzinger, nos. 1525, 1541.

14. "Just as the Word is flesh in the flesh, so man is God in God."

15. William Styron, *Set This House on Fire*, p. 379.

16. Thomas Aquinas, *Summa Theologica*, II–II, 13, 3, ad 1.

17. Thomas Aquinas, *Summa Contra Gentiles*, 3, 71.

7

The Christian Vision
of Eternal Life:
Man Is Not Alone

The vast multitude of persons on earth reveals to man that there are real, immediate things for him to do. All men confront the same basic choice about whether they will use their intelligence and talents in the service of one another. Clearly, this involves the eventual and total transformation of the world for man, as we have already seen. In the beginning, man is not given everything. He is given merely the power to act by himself. What he does with his capacity, how he utilizes it, is up to his experience, knowledge and freedom. The choice God gives to man is a free choice. It is in the finite context of his love and responsibilities for others whom he actually does see. "Anyone who says 'I love God,' and hates his brother, is a liar, since the man who does not love the brother that he can see cannot love God, whom he has never seen." (1 John 4:20)

God's choice presented to man is a free choice because, as we have seen, he chose to associate other persons with him in his eternal life.

In His goodness and wisdom, God chose to reveal Himself and
to make known to us the hidden purpose of His will (cf. Eph.
1:9) by which through Christ, the Word made flesh, man has
access to the Father in the Holy Spirit and comes to share in
the divine nature (cf. Eph. 2:18; 2 Pet. 1:4). Through this revelation, therefore, the invisible God (cf. Col. 1:15; 1 Tim. 1:17) out
of the abundance of His love speaks to men as friends (cf. Ex.
33:11; Jn. 15:14–15) and lives among them (cf. Bar. 3:38), so
that He may invite and take them into fellowship with Himself.[1]

Persons, then, are autonomous, they cannot be coerced and
still remain persons. What God wanted were persons who
actually loved one another in freedom. This is the basic point in
his creation and redemption.

God is present to men most particularly when they are
thinking responsibly and acting energetically to solve the
problems before them; at such times their pleas for divine
help are most efficacious. Indeed passive faith which contents
itself with sterile inactivity, with the hope that everything
will turn out well no matter what men do, is not even
Christian. God is not on the side of those who do not act
when action is called for. The mission of Christianity is not
exclusively, then, to "save men's souls," as if this were somehow possible apart from man's responsibility to the world.
Indolence in the face of inhuman social conditions, injustice,
prejudice—such failures to be fully human can condemn a
man as irrevocably as a deliberate denial of revelation.

The public life of man is what is most visible to us. He
raises buildings and writes poems, sings songs, paints pictures.
When we want to know whether man has been present in

any area, we look for surviving traces of these things. These are the passing efforts by which man defies time, which linger on in the world beyond his lifetime and tell us who or what he was. These cultural evidences also reveal how different men can be from one another—how diverse are the ways of singing, writing, painting, dancing and governing. Any visit to a museum devoted to the history of locomotion, or pottery or human dress leaves the lasting impression of man's long, slow, incredible effort to improve and to decorate himself and what he makes. He learns in time, in gradual steps. He learns that there are many different ways to do the same thing, many ways of being a man.

The immense variety among the products of men might well be expected merely as a deduction from nature itself, where variation is the almost bewildering concomitant of development. But the variety of man is even more striking since it is deliberate. Man's memory, his knowledge of his own history, precludes any mere duplication of the past: he is not bound to what he has already done, except as a source of knowledge and experience.

THE MEANING OF CIVIL LIFE

For Aristotle, man was the being whose distinctive characteristic was political life. This does not mean that man had no higher purpose beyond political life, but that what especially distinguished him was his mode of procedure in the city. The visible social and political creation was, in other words, the special sphere of the human.

The fundamental element in political life as such is the

development of justice. Man stands today at a point in history where he can reasonably hope to create a society wherein all men can expect to live a full human life, and this despite the challenges presented by overpopulation, poverty, and the slowness of economic development in the backward countries. The basic economic and social life required by man as a foundation for his physical life on earth is within the realm of possibility. It is, as we have said, an invitation. The achieving of some real level of social life for all men lies at the foundation of all higher things in human life. In this sense, the first thing man must do is to establish a reign of justice within his social units and international life.[2]

FRIENDSHIP AND THE END OF HUMAN LIFE

Politics is the order of justice. It seeks a limited, finite, adequate society for man on earth. It joins men together in a life with common projects, common goals. Politics is worthwhile, indeed fundamental for man. Yet politics is itself a means to something else. The purpose of politics, of justice, is friendship. And friendship is the point at which men really meet God in this life. God, in his inner life, is not alone. The life of friendship is where man is not alone. It is for this reason that man is ultimately created, for friendship with his fellow men and with God. Thus politics, having created a public society in which man can achieve a normal amount of security and dignity, still leaves man impoverished, aloof, even in this life, if politics is taken to be the absolute end of man's life. Politics, of course, cannot legislate friendship, for friendship is the product of freedom and choice. Nevertheless the stable, growing order it creates makes friendships possible among men. This is the highest destiny of politics.

We have not, therefore, penetrated to the depth of man's social nature if we content ourselves with establishing a society in which men are made—or better, allowed to make themselves—good citizens. Even if, when death comes, they have reached natural perfection in the sense of well-ordered lives, is this enough? We must look further. There is something beyond this kind of virtue, and that is precisely friendship, the true perfection society itself produces.

The philosophy of love and friendship is at the root of society. It is the goal of any real human life in the city. There are two classical ways of distinguishing the different kinds of friendship: (1) according to the kind of communication involved and (2) according to the basis and end of the friendship—that is, utility, pleasure, or virtue. Of course, friendship based on virtue is best, but we should not fail to understand the importance of friendship based on business or pleasure. These two make human life more agreeable and enjoyable. For instance, the purchase of a book or an article of clothing from a large store may be just a communication which is complete if both parties are satisfied with the sale. Suppose, however, a clerk sees the customer coming, greets him with a smile and shows real interest in him and in his purchase. The two have a pleasant conversation over the article itself or about a variety of other topics. The customer then leaves the store and the two may never see each other again. Yet that exchange was a fine thing, it made something otherwise a matter of routine or even distasteful into a pleasant human encounter. Society as a whole benefited, as did both men, because there was real friendliness here, based on utility, to be sure, but still the kind of relationship which lessens the tensions among men. Such friendly communications can also be the starting point of the more perfect type of friendship and a closer union among the members of society.

The perfection of all human communication is friendship based on virtue, that is, on those things that are most uniquely human. A man who is, theoretically, perfectly good will be unhappy without a friend. For as we know, man's true happiness is not in the simple possession of a number of fine qualities, but in the joyful exercise of his powers. And the distinguishing characteristic of friendship, that which sets it apart from other activities, is that it involves the communication to another of one's highest powers. Thus the phrase of Scripture that it is not good for man to be alone is not solely pertinent to the man-wife relationship; in a sense it applies to every human relationship. The society of friends, then, is established and secured through the communication between men of the realities of their natures.

In true friendship, above all, man lives most fully, since here human faculties are exercised to the full. Friendship implies that we come closest to the being and life of a friend precisely when we communicate thoughts, ideas, projects, and choices, for this is what naturally relates us to the other person in his true life. If our friend is a good person, the highest manifestation of his being, his thoughts and his loves, will be most delightful to us. We need our friends, then, even for our very human endeavors, for friendship is what makes us what we are.

So it is that the principal act of friendship is what Aquinas called *convivere,* which consists in the communication in a shared life of human ideas and ideals. Such is the primary human stimulus to contemplation as well as the basic source of the new and vital thinking required for the continuous development of a people. The joy and comradeship of friends is, then, found in their intercommunication itself. ". . . True friendship desires to see the friend and causes a rejoicing in much conversation, towards which end friendship is principally ordained . . . "[3] Thus there is a truth of the most profound nature in the observation that "the supreme and ultimate product of civilization . . . is two or three persons talking together in a room."[4] Society depends for its vitality on its ability to effect or encourage friendships among its members. Aquinas, who understood the importance of friendship so well, rightly remarked that ". . . all precepts of law, especially those ordered to the neighbor, seem to be ordained to this end, that men love one another."[5]

The love of friendship is required by society because it alone of its very nature makes a society a real relation between persons. Real communication must be a sharing of love and life by rational beings. The ultimate and most perfect meaning of society, then, will be the interaction of men who are friends. Of course natural justice and friendship, even of the highest sort, are simply not sufficient to men: any intelligent understanding of human nature will tell us that another dimension is needed for human nature to overcome the insufficiency of motivation and the lack of universal love which we find at the root of all social friction. At this point, however, we do not wish to treat Christianity from the aspect of eternal life and ultimate friendship with God, since we shall be doing this later in this chapter; rather we wish to suggest its importance in earthly society.

The three major failings of natural society appear to be: (1) the inability to make men good, (2) the inability to extend love and friendship to all men, and (3) the inability to order rightly men's interior intentions as well as their external conditions and dispositions.[6] All societal evils can ultimately be placed under one or more of these heads. It is only the Christian law which does not cease at the external act, but passes beyond to order correctly man's interior acts and ideas, placing order at the very root of the matter. Further, since man is a social being needing other men, this relationship is most adequately attained by a mutual and sincere love which binds all men to one another. Thus, the divine law is meant as a help to the natural order, which itself demands that men respect and love one another. Men usually help one another when they can. It is this natural tendency that must be supported against the too brutal Hobbesian view of human nature as always involving war between men. It can be said, then, that a society of Christian men should come the closest to a perfect civil body on earth, since among them the sources of friction and hatred can be most completely recognized and controlled, while the sources of human and divine love are most effectively encouraged and in operation.

In this whole matter of friendship and its perfection in the communication of thoughts and ideals, of dreams and hopes, we very often, it seems, permit ourselves to be confused and deceived. We live our lives as if these friendships were mere incidents or side issues to the main problems of existence. But the reality is quite otherwise. We live our lives for our friendships; they are the goals, not the means. Sometimes it seems as if the only modern man who really saw this truth as it is was G. K. Chesterton, who in this as in so many things communicated his vision in a most interesting and unique way. Indeed Chesterton's book on Charles Dickens is perhaps the best societal analysis ever written. The concluding lines summarize the meaning and perfection of friendship in human life:

The hour of absinthe is over. We shall not be much further troubled with the little artists who found Dickens too sane for their sorrows and too clean for their delights. But we have a long way to travel before we get back to what Dickens meant: and the passage is along a rambling English road, a twisting road such as Mr. Pickwick travelled. But this at least is part of what he meant; that comradeship and serious joy are not interludes in our travel; but that rather our travels are interludes in comradeship and joy, which through God shall endure for ever. The inn does not point to the road; the road points to the inn. And all roads point at last to an ultimate inn, where we shall meet Dickens and all his characters; and when we drink again it shall be from the great flagons in the tavern at the end of the world.[7]

And again we see that the vision of Christianity has not been wrong in proclaiming that the friendships of men are the very means to the friendship with our God—he who loves his neighbor has fulfilled the law. So too, when Christ Our Lord wished to show his Apostles his deep love for them, he could only say to them, "I shall not call you servants any more . . . I call you friends, because I have made known to you everything I have learnt from my Father." (John 15:15) And here we have it! God sharing his ideas and ideals with men—this is indeed the highest and most perfect act of friendship possible to us, his creatures.

THE CONSEQUENCES OF FRIENDSHIP

The discovery of who we are is ultimately bound up with the discovery of another person. And the real discovery of another always contains an element of surprise, is always potentially a friendship, always means a breaking through of our own narrowness and limitation. Man confronts the world which stands before him as something plastic, pliable, capable of being transformed by his activity. Through his meeting with the world he meets other persons who share the life of the world with him. Somehow man recognizes that it is by participation in this real world wherein he meets other persons that he returns to the ultimate reality. In this sense, individualism is further from the true reality than collectivism, which at least recognizes an absolute outside the self—something individualism fails to do.

Man, the individual, is not sufficient to himself. This is a primary insight; indeed it is the basis of any honest appreciation of oneself. Man experiences not his own absoluteness but rather his own limitation, his finiteness. At the same time, however, the desire somehow to get back to, or to grasp, the infinite is the driving force of the finite person. The real question is the nature of man's return to God. And it is here, in the meaning of speech, of man's personal communion with others in friendship, that the self is most fully discovered.

Individuals have ideas and feelings, they experience reality in their personal being, but it is only when the person sees himself reflected in the life of another—in a common solidarity with some men and all men—that he begins to perceive again wherein the absolute lies. We discover not merely ourselves, but also the infinite and absolute when, through communication in love and knowledge with other men, we become oriented to a reality beyond ourselves. "Where two or three meet in my name, I shall be there with them." (Matthew 18:20)

This is why John asked how one who does not love his brother, whom he sees, can love God whom he does not see. And the reason John so insisted upon this is that "love comes from God, and everyone who loves is begotten by God and knows God" (1 John 4:7). Hence, love of your neighbor is no arbitrary command but belongs to reality itself, for God is in the midst of our human relationships when there is in them a true communication of knowledge and love. In the dispensation of grace in which we live, all love is from God, and the whole of man's being is called to love. The insight, at times so vivid to us, that knowledge and love are not wholly transient, that our very recognition of the limitations in them is somehow essentially connected with limitlessness, is enough to convince us that the discovery of who we are is really the progressive discovery of others; that without such relationships of knowledge and love the self is denuded of meaning.

But our discovery of who we are cannot be complete until we discover the ultimate object towards which the knowledge and love we somehow sense as limitless tend: until we discover that absoluteness itself, the source of the cosmos we confront, is Another, capable of knowing and being known, loving and being loved. The ultimate revelation to man is that God himself is not alone, that he is triune; that the personal life of God is other-oriented.

Here, in the One who is self-sufficient in the highest order of being and knowledge and love, is the resolution of the insufficiency we experience in ourselves in the here and now. Here we shall find not only the fulfillment of our quest for reality but the guarantee that the knowledge and love of our friends, so fleeting in life, yet so permanent in desire, shall endure forever.

THE CHRISTIAN VISION OF ETERNAL LIFE

Society, culture, civilization—all these realities and creations of mankind—are real only in the persons who make them live, who bear their reality in their own persons at any given moment of time. As each generation passes on man is always brought face to face with the abiding fear that what is of real import in his experience—what seemingly the world is all about, the personal lives of men—is everywhere eventually defeated in the case of each person by his death.

Yet the defeat represented by death in the individual appears to be a positive value with regard to the generations. Room is made for others, new minds, new changes, new developments. The world itself is not such that one lifetime or one generation is enough to discover all that it can reveal to man of his meaning and his task. This greater mission to deal with the totality of the world belongs to the whole race throughout time.

The individual man who confronts the world he is in for

an allotted span of time is up against the great paradox of the seeming contrast between his experience and his certitude that he too will die. He is bound to ask himself about the validity and worth of his friendships, his commitments, his tasks. Is there anything that can give ground to his belief or hope that this temporal world is not in fact the end?

Man recognizes, first of all, that the tendencies and operations by which he knows, senses, chooses, and acts are all "given" to him. The operational structures and processes of sight or hearing, for example, simply work. They are not the constructed result of some lately discovered scientific theory, as the computer is; they are the result of a man's simply opening his eyes and seeing, or turning his ear and listening. Neither did man, before he chose something, decide to give himself the power of choice. The procedure was simply there in his personal being. Moreover, the coordination of different sensory and intellectual faculties, the faculties themselves, and their normal operations are discovered by man to be present within himself operating in a unified manner. Man is thus forced outside himself by his most intimate powers and operations, for they are presented to him, as it were, he did not himself construct them in his own personal being. They are, in short, natural to him.

Thought is a personal attribute of a thinking being, it does not exist outside a rational mind. The reflective mind, the mind which sees itself thinking, can empirically distinguish in its own operations what originates in the source of knowledge and what originates in the knower. The human person, however, experiences himself as a whole, as a unit which discovers that even his own inclinations to live, to know, and to love are original tendencies given to him as an integral part of his own total givenness. Man knows that he did not create himself, or his tendencies, or the peculiarities of their functioning within himself. Nor did he discover them from someone else. No man first recognized his own personal desire to preserve his own life in a textbook of ethics or of philosophy. The desire to know in man is not the result but the cause of his education. These are initial experiences, present in man before they are intellectually formalized.

But this analysis leads further. Even after we recognize that we do have basic drives, that we do seek for a permanence beyond death, that we do formulate some sort of intellectual concept about what it means to live and to know, we are not satisfied with this knowledge as such. For it is not knowledge alone that can ultimately satisfy us. We always seek out *presence*, we seek to go out to that "other" which we know to be the origin of knowledge. We are fundamentally interested in life itself, not merely in our knowledge of it. We seek to know "face to face," as it were, in all things. In other words, knowledge always refers to its sources. And the source of knowledge can only be possessed in a concrete, living action. We experience ourselves, then, as persons using our knowledge in order to attain that other which is the source of our knowledge. And this drive of knowledge is always essentially contemplative; that is, it does not seek to destroy the thing known, but to behold it, to be with it, to share its life.

The process of time, however, reveals to us that we must continue to choose, to grasp by singular acts various real beings which present themselves to us. Yet each act as it happens in a lifetime does attain some worthwhile purpose, some answer to some tendency we find in ourselves. Thus we perceive that only through choices and actions elicited in a world of others can we hope to rise out of our confinement. We experience our own insufficiency. But we also experience real tendencies in our being; we concretely experience that some tendencies are satisfied by real objects. Nevertheless, we know that we did not create these tendencies in ourselves, nor the objects that satisfy them, nor the interrelation between the object and the tendency.

This experience is consequently of such fundamental import that it requires us to posit another relationship. We do discover in ourselves a tendency to some object, some reality, that can satisfy all our tendencies. But this tendency is also a "given," with a status no less mysterious than that of any other of the experienced tendencies. Thus, just as in the operations of the other tendencies we seek their fulfillment in some object of reality outside ourselves, so in the case of this tendency we seek its fulfillment outside ourselves. The ultimate meaning of human choice in time, then, is connected with the pursuit of this "other" in a living, concrete act.

THE MEANING OF THE RESURRECTION

This is where revelation meets and answers our human questioning. Christianity teaches man that he can accept the very fact of death as a prelude to union, in ultimate friendship, with that "Other" who is the source of his knowledge, that Other towards whom his whole being finally tends; that this drive for totality corresponds with what man is *for;* it is that to which he is directed by God's intention for him. Christianity, in other words, teaches, as the Creed affirms, the resurrection of the body and life everlasting. There is nothing as crucial to the world or to man as this central reality of Christianity—that the Son of God became man at a given point of time—during the administration of Pontius Pilate and Herod—that this same Son of God was crucified and died, that he rose again from the dead and ascended into heaven, where he intercedes for us eternally in his glorified humanity, as the Son-made-man. Mankind is invited to follow Christ, not with any utopia in view, but, as Hebrews so beautifully relates, through the realities of this world, through death itself, to resurrection. (Hebrews 5:1–10) The consequences of the Fall, the results of human choice, God has not removed. The divine response to man's free choice was the redemption *according to the flesh*.

Be it noted that the major objection to this doctrine of the Resurrection is not that it is a contradiction of human desires and hopes, for it is in accord with them. Rather, Christianity is, so to speak, its own worst intellectual enemy precisely because in the eyes of the world the doctrine of the resurrection of man, body and soul, into eternal life is too good to be true, too perfect a fulfillment of man's most basic needs—his need of an absolutely free choice of his personal destiny; his need of a meaningful task in the world that is determinative of this destiny; his need for redemption; his need to believe that his own personal life is itself without end because in loving others on this earth he has experienced a presentiment of a love which never has an end. Indeed it is precisely on the basis of man's primary experience of permanence—his experience of friendship—that he is promised resurrection into everlasting life, into the life of God. The meaning of the Resurrection is that God's choice to invite others in his creation to share his life includes the invitation of the whole human person, the whole reality of what a man is.

We have seen that the world and its tasks are the vital center of man's vocation; that the fulfillment of his earthly mission and the possibility of his salvation depend on the efforts he expends towards the transformation of the world in the service of other men. We have seen, too, that the point at which the atheist's convictions are most strongly reinforced is where Christians and other believers undervalue or even ignore man's earthly task. And yet it seems as if the prime danger in our time were not that the world will not somehow be transformed into a more technically perfect place for man to live in but that this transformation in the name of man's earthly task will entail his loss of freedom. The abiding fear which possesses the more thoughtful minds among our contemporaries comes from modern man's readiness to believe that a sufficiency of this world's goods will solve all his problems.

We are assured that mankind now has it within its power to eliminate hunger, poverty, and disease. A little investigation into demography, economic development projections, statistics of international agriculture and natural resources, educational and medical requirements gives us a working estimate of national and world needs. We can even calculate what is likely to be done country by country across the globe to meet these needs. In the order of knowledge, we appear to have a total grasp of what there is to be done.

On the surface of international life, the conclusion mankind should draw from such investigations seems at first simple and obvious. The greatest number of these temporal problems can be solved—provided that the full force of leadership and effort be brought to bear upon them. Is it not then utterly illogical, some say, if not insane, that political or religious or ideological divisions among men should keep them from seeing that they can remake the world in the image of man's welfare?

More and more nations, this argument runs, are spending their major energies in developing military systems complete with ever more destructive hydrogen weapons and ever more effective delivery apparatus. Some ten to twenty nations will soon possess them. Out of the mere existence of these weapons a war is certain to result, with much of civilization being destroyed. *No* ideal is worth this disaster. *Therefore*—the analysis pushes on to its inescapable conclusion—we must disarm; we must efface the ideological differences that make arms necessary, bypass the political leaders responsible for our conditions, and work together for universal peace and prosperity before civilization is wiped out. Let us dismantle our weapons! Let us use our resources to help the poor, to relieve suffering. Let us condemn out of hand these ideas and philosophies and religions which are divisive, which stand in the way of universal human brotherhood! The logic here, it seems, is iron, unbreakable.

Yet somehow we are not wholly convinced. It is characteristic of the perplexities of our day that the conclusions of our best thinkers, of many of our most committed people, seem to us to be merely private opinions. We are able to follow their reasoning, we even perhaps see that what they are saying is true. But in the end we do not *believe* it. And we live by our beliefs more than by our reasonings. We have a vague feeling that we are missing some element vital to attaining certitude in these matters.

Somewhere in the back of the mind is the recollection that in the old ideologies and religions out of which our modern world grew, men waged wars to prove that there are issues in human life more basic than food, health, and security. Men, so it was believed, could be full, healthy, and safe, and yet be inhuman. Our dim memories and suspicions that such might still be the case are still strong enough to prevent us from totally dismantling our weapons and discharging our soldiers. This presentiment may be a remnant of primitive man in the unconscious, as many think, but it may also be a valid fear, one based on human reality—something we cannot afford to take the chance of ignoring because of the disastrous effects of being wrong.

Here, it seems, we are face to face with an issue that transcends the normal levels of our thinking. Indeed, whenever any argument seems totally clear and rational, yet finally unacceptable to common sense, we are forced to wonder whether we are not dealing with the realm commonly called "mystery," with a category that has to do, not with our scientific constructs, but with our destiny and purposes as men.

The arguments for disarmament with the hope of abolishing worldwide hunger and disease do not gain the immediate acceptance they logically deserve because they are all too frequently expressions of a concept of human values which the majority of people reject. The great majority of people cannot believe that our freedom is not somehow involved here and that our freedom is not worth fighting for. The failure to take into account this flickering element of doubt is what makes the programs for world peace lose their argumentative force. In the last analysis, man does not live by bread alone. His right to die for his beliefs if necessary, to prefer civilization to food, is ultimately what makes him to be man.

The dogmas of Christian theology are often surprisingly relevant in the most unexpected places. Here we have been examining the implications of what is undoubtedly the major intellectual phenomenon of our times, the elevation of human "life"—life in the sense of food, clothing, shelter, recreation, health, in short the "good life"—into the status of the major value of human society. Against the criterion of the good life, all other values seem to yield their primacy. Our age, faced with a choice between liberty or peace and security, almost unquestioningly chooses the latter. The continuation of "life," physical, terrestrial life, as long as possible has become, as Hannah Arendt has pointed out, the idol which topples governments and civilizations which do not worship at it.

Such a view seems to motivate much of our peace philosophy. It moved a former president of Brazil to warn:

We Latin Americans are now in a phase where we either definitely enter economic prosperity or nobody will detain the wave of despair of millions of human beings who no longer accept the limited conditions of life in which they vegetate, because they now realize that there are ways of escaping misery.[8]

The stress on the primacy of life tends to reinforce Arnold Toynbee's analysis:

> The doctrine underlying the Russo-American economic ideology is that free enterprise (or communism) has turned America (or Russia) into an earthly paradise in which "all is for the best in the best of all possible worlds." In an earthly paradise there is not, of course, room for sickness or sorrow. Consequently, any wretched human being is being guilty of something like high treason.
>
> This is hard, indeed. For the inevitable ills of life are bad enough in themselves and, if they involve the sufferer in becoming a criminal as well, this is almost an intolerable aggravation of them. Something like this is entailed in an economic ideology of either the American or Russian variety because each assumes that a particular economic system brings the millennium with it.[9]

If we recall that in the history of thought the origin of economics is related to the secularization of the idea of salvation, we can better appreciate how the primacy of life can reign supreme in the minds of many of our contemporaries, how the economy can offer a security that God could not.

THE RESURRECTION: JUDGMENT AND HOPE

Into this context which concentrates all too exclusively on the welfare man can acquire for himself in this life appears, astonishingly enough, the dogma of the resurrection of the flesh, perhaps the most dynamic and vital element in the whole movement of modern Christian thought. That the Resurrection lies at the foundation of Christian belief is obvious from its very inception. Christ is risen! We shall rise again with him! We believe in the God who has raised Christ. Without the Resurrection, our faith is vain. Thus our salvation is not radically our own work but depends upon the Passion-Resurrection-Pentecost cycle of the Lord. Ultimately, we are saved; mankind does not save itself.

The Resurrection, consequently, is also, as Karl Barth rightly insisted, a judgment of this world. He who believes in this resurrection cannot promise men that they can fulfill by themselves all their needs and desires in this life by political or economic or military or artistic means. The dogma of the Resurrection precisely says that the millennium is not here, that man's ultimate desires can only be completed beyond this life within the life of God, that the hope or promise of achieving them here is by definition idolatry, the belief that man has in his power the capability of satisfying *all* his desires by himself.

From this, it appears at once obvious why we must inquire into what actually motivates our belief that we can in fact solve man's problems of disarmament, hunger, disease, and security. We must be virtually aware of what exactly we are proposing. Oftentimes but a thin thread separates doctrines that strive to alleviate the hunger of the body and those that attempt also to fill the hunger of the soul. Indeed, in communism, in much of the socialism envisioned by the leaders of developing countries, in various forms of liberal, conservative or atheistic humanism, there is a virtual identity of the two. Through such a unification, the fulfillment of the needs of life and the good life tends to become the true and mystical mission of mankind itself.

THE CHRISTIAN DILEMMA: THIS WORLD OR THE NEXT?

Here, if anywhere, Christians are confronted with one of the deepest and most agonizing dilemmas of their theology, the conflict between the obligations of this world and the next, and in what sense these two are related, as the Christian must believe that they are. Christians are the first to agree with Pierre and Peggy Streit's profoundly human concern which wonders "why we are blessed." Why have we Americans and Europeans so much, while the rest of the world seems to have so little? Christians must agree "that apart from preserving the peace, the first, overriding, frighteningly pressing task of this year and this century is to feed, clothe and unleash from fear the nations who, through no fault of their own, live in such desolation."[10] Nevertheless, in spite of the sometimes formidable evidence that belief in the Resurrection has in specific cultures and places lessened enthusiasm and devotion to the pressing tasks of this world, Christians would betray their vocation to man if they should contribute to the illusion that perhaps this is all there is, that the mission of man is really only the feeding, the clothing, the sheltering of men in this life—this and nothing more.

The great Christian problem, to return again to a theme we have so often touched upon in these pages, is simply stated: What is there remaining for man to do in this world precisely as Christian man? For many of the early Christians, all was already accomplished with the Resurrection. Salvation was achieved in Christ. Only a short time remained. Vigils were organized in preparation for the advent of the Bridegroom. As time passed, however, and the Parousia did not come, Christians began to turn back and reflect on the teachings of the Lord, on the parables of the Mustard Seed and the Harvest and the Kingdom. They began to realize with Paul that the exact extent of the time between the Ascension and the Second Coming would be a long one, that their failure to preach to all the cities of Galilee before the return of the Lord might in fact contain the literal truth.

Our Lord "consummated" his work. His own words bear witness to this. (John 19:30) So the work of the Lord, the radical salvation of men, was completed. The "latter times" had begun. Mankind was redeemed. The People of God could now hope to reach the abiding presence of the Godhead, could hope to live his life. The resurrection of the flesh! Who is really more astounded by this belief? The Jew? to whom it is a scandal. The Greek? to whom it is merely foolish. Or ourselves? to whom it is rather too good actually to be true, too incomprehensible to think about clearly. Yet this is the doctrine by which the world is judged.

What remains to be done? To this question the dogma of the resurrection of the flesh comes like a mighty wind clearing the atmosphere of the mind. For it alone tells man the limits and purposes of his political and cultural life—what he can and what he cannot expect from this earth. It teaches that man is mortal, that he can only expect what is humanly feasible, and that whatever is achieved—even the elimination of hunger, poverty, and disease—will fall short of producing a man who will not in the end suffer and die. It affirms that man does in truth have desires which reach beyond his temporal needs. This very truth exempts politics, economics, technology and culture from the false demand that they by themselves should be able to meet man's ultimate problems. Freed from issues beyond their competence, they can be used for what they really are—practical, workable devices and procedures in the temporal city, skills and methods that can improve the lot of the halt and the lame and the blind without enslaving their minds in the process of emancipation. In short, man can be treated as the finite creature he really is, yet the creature who is destined to eternal life.

What, then, remains for the Christian to do? We are assigned two precisely Christian missions while on earth: in Matthew, the making of disciples of all nations by baptizing them and teaching all that was commanded; in Paul, the delivery of all creation to the freedom of the Sons of God. Here, in teaching what was commanded and in restoring creation, the Christian finds what remains for him to do. "For I was hungry and you gave me food; I was thirsty . . . a stranger . . . naked . . . sick or in prison . . ." such are the commands. (Cf. Matthew 25:39-40.) And today we have seen how this is not possible for all men unless we renew the face of the earth by what we know, so that the fruits of the earth can reach all. Holiness and sanctification for the Christian mean involvement in this work. This is the mission—to preach to all nations that our salvation does not lie in this life, yet is achieved only through this life, through renewing this world in which we dwell, through our relationship with one another. The tasks of this world are Christian tasks.

The resurrection of the flesh is, therefore, a dogma of the greatest contemporary relevance, shedding its light on all we attempt for the elimination of the world's hunger and poverty. For if we pursue this task as idolaters, as men who preach to the poor that we can fulfill their ultimate needs with our skills, our goods and our inventions, we are deceivers and even destroyers. But when we face the crisis of world poverty, hunger, and need in the spirit of the Christian mission to the world, we take our place beside our contemporaries armed with a criterion whereby we can more readily sift the true possibilities for aid and peace from among those which are false and vain. If the men of our time are looking for ultimate answers in politics and economics and culture, we must part company with them, because we know that final solutions are not to be found there. We would betray mankind were we to pretend otherwise. But if men are willing to recognize the limited and transient nature of human life, the agonizing delays and vexing tangles which inevitably beset all human progress, then we can help. Indeed, we must. We will do all we can, and then, beyond welfare and security and the good life, lies the Resurrection. We diminish man by promising him anything less. The first and last freedom for the Christian is precisely the freedom to affirm that this best of all possible worlds is not enough. This, in the end, is what the resurrection of the flesh, today as yesterday, means to humanity.

THE END OF CREATION: ETERNAL LIFE

Beyond the Resurrection lies eternal life. The life of God is now shared with all those who have chosen him. This is the City of God of which Augustine spoke. "Meanwhile, and always, the City of God is everlasting and perfect peace, and not merely a continuing peace which individually mortal men enter upon and leave by birth and death, but one in which individuals immortally abide. . . ."[11] The universe achieves its purpose through the persons who have accepted the invitation to live the life of the Trinity. As St. Paul says, the whole of creation is to be redeemed by Christ. It is not to be annihilated, as has on occasion been inferred from a rather hasty reading of some apocalyptic traditions. In principle, the cosmos is to share in the glory of the Resurrection. "Then will come the time of the restoration of all things (Acts 3:21). Then the human race as well as the entire world, which is intimately related to man and achieves its purpose through him, will be perfectly re-established in Christ (cf. Eph. 1:10; Col. 1:20; 2 Pet. 3:10–13)."[12]

The whole point of the Resurrection is that man does *not* cease to be man. As man, furthermore, he is directly related to the universe. He is simply unthinkable without this relationship to the world even in the risen life. Indeed the uniqueness of Christianity, in its teaching of everlasting life, is that it is not a belief in the mere immortality of the soul, or in absorption into the infinite, or in the eternal return. It is a belief in the permanence of the whole human person. Christ in his glorified humanity stands before the Father making intercession for us. His resurrection is a promise of ours.

MAN'S END: WITH GOD

Much has been written about the loneliness of modern man in a world wherein the progress of science and culture has seemed to create divisions among men and to isolate the individual. There is a real sense, of course, in which the Christian does not belong to this world of loneliness and unbelief. The believer simply does not know experimentally what it is not to believe. He does not know what it is, in that sense, to be alone in this world. This is oftentimes not too well understood. It is worth spelling out in some detail.

In the Christian view a man who does not believe is held to be nevertheless an object of God's salvific will. He is not yet a public member of the visible community through which grace and *agape* are dispensed. Yet in some fashion, obscure to us but no less real, this man is being sought out by God, a search in which God mysteriously uses other men. Likewise, the unbeliever on his part is also inevitably a searcher. He is a man who does not know the structure of reality or its effects upon him. This is his personal problem. His actions and choices in life are expressions at one level or another of his effort to define who he is and whether he is ultimately alone.

The pattern of life which such a man may follow, being deficient in the ordinary channels of grace, motivation, and order, will quite often lead through situations and encounters which in a Christian sense might be defined as objective sin and scandal. But this so-called objective sin, even when culpable—that is, even when it is a concrete denial of the love which the person should have for another in creation—never stands outside the search of man for a meaning. Nor—of greater importance—does it stand outside God's effort to bring good out of evil and grace out of life. The Christian who is content to judge his unbelieving contemporary on the surface will hopelessly fail to comprehend the problem of unbelief.

But the question of man's aloneness is not merely a problem of isolation; even more it is a question of whether man contains within himself the sources and resources necessary to make himself and the world meaningful. Is man, in the final reckoning, an adequate center for science, art, politics, or history? When we pose such a question in the present context, we touch upon something which, more than anything else, serves to highlight the place of Christianity in the present world. For Christianity, we have suggested, makes a thoroughly unique claim, a claim whose breadth and scope is almost never fully comprehended. The claim is this—that man is not alone, that the totality of history and science has an order entirely compatible with dogma, that man is the center but not the maker of the created universe, that the destiny of man is, in the end, to be with God, to live the life of the Trinity. The practical manifestation of this claim means that a man can be a Christian and anything else—a biologist, an historian, a painter, a physicist, a sociologist, an astronomer—with no fear or possibility of contradiction. Faith and beauty and truth are one. The unrecognized truth of our time is the paradox that only the religious believer still maintains the unity of scientific, historical, and religious reality.

Once we have understood this feeling about the aloneness of man in the world, an aloneness which tends to turn man back on himself in search of meaning, we who are Christians can better appreciate why Christianity must sound so strange to our contemporaries. This strangeness of Christianity does not stem primarily from its so-called antiquarianism or the legalism of its law. Rather, it lies deeper, in the essential dogmas of the faith, in the Trinity and the Incarnation, in eternal life which is the ultimate and definitive Christian response to the aloneness of man. As we have said before, they seem too good to be true. Perhaps no more joyous human response to our faith exists than that of Hopkins:

Man, how fast his firedint, his mark on mind, is gone!
Both are in an unfathomable, all is in an enormous dark
Drowned. O pity and indignation! Manshape, that shone
Sheer off, disseveral, a star, death blots black out; not mark
            Is any of him at all so stark
But vastness blurs and time beats level. Enough! the Resurrection,
A heart's-clarion! Away grief's gasping, joyless days, dejection.
            Across my foundering deck shone
A beacon, an eternal beam. Flesh fade, and mortal trash
Fall to the residuary worm; world's wildfire, leave but ash:
            In a flash, at a trumpet crash,
I am all at once what Christ is, since he was what I am, and
This Jack, joke, poor potsherd, patch, matchwood, immortal dia-
    mond,
            Is immortal diamond.[13]

The concrete destiny of each living man, then, is immortal diamond, is to live the life of the Trinity, eternal life wherein man meets the meaning of reality, meets reality itself, in community, in fellowship with the persons who live the common life of God.

In much of the apologetics of the past, the stress on personal salvation has played a great part. This, of course, is basic to the faith, important at all times. Yet it seems that the end product of salvation, the reality of eternal life, has been insufficiently considered. This is especially true in our age, which is primarily concerned, not with the sense of sin, but with a sense of finiteness, of aloneness, and of the finality of death. At the center of modern man's loneliness is the suspicion that the universe is only man in some other form, that this is all there is. If the Christian is to meet the world of his time in any meaningful sense, it must be at the point where this world ends, in death; and where Christianity begins, with eternal life in which man finds his fulfillment and the explanation of his meaning. As Augustine says:

God will be the source of every satisfaction, more than any heart can rightly crave, more than life and health, food and wealth, glory and honor, peace and every good—so that God, as St. Paul said, "may be all in all" (1 Corinthians, 15:28). He will be the consummation of all our desiring—the object of our unending vision, of our unlessening love, of our unwearying praise. And in this gift of vision, this response of love, this paean of praise, all alike will share in everlasting life.[14]

For man, this destiny can only come as a glorious surprise, beyond all his expectations. For it is a total gift that can only be opened on the appointed day when all the things man secretly hopes might be true are presented to him forever, when he realizes that he and his fellows really are with one another, with the triune God. So it is that the Christian vision of the world ends, as Paul tells us, in vision itself. In the end, all is light.

NOTES

1. "Dogmatic Constitution on Divine Revelation," *The Documents of Vatican II*, ed. Walter Abbott, no. 2, p. 112.

2. This again is the purport of *Mater et Magistra, Pacem in Terris,* "The Church in the Modern World," and *Populorum Progressio.*

3. Thomas Aquinas, *III Sentences*, d. 27, q. 2, a. 1, ad 11.

4. Cited in George Herbert Palmer, *Self-Cultivation in English* (Boston: Houghton Mifflin, 1909), p. 6.

5. Thomas Aquinas, *Summa Theologica*, I–II, 105, 2, ad 1.

6. Cf. I–II, 91, 4.

7. G. K. Chesterton, *Charles Dickens* (New York: Dodd, Mead & Co., 1906).

8. Cited in *The New York Times*, January 1, 1961, p. 15. Cf. also Hannah Arendt, *The Human Condition* (Garden City, N.Y.: Doubleday Anchor, 1959).

9. Arnold Toynbee, "Spiritual Freedom Is the Great Difference," *The New York Times Magazine*, January 15, 1961, p. 30. © 1961 by The New York Times Company. Reprinted by permission.

10. Pierre and Peggy Streit, "Basic Query: Why Are We Blessed?" *The New York Times Magazine*, January 8, 1961, p. 70.

11. St. Augustine, *The City of God*, G. G. Walsh et al. (Garden City, N.Y.: Doubleday Image, 1958), Book XIX, p. 468.

12. "Dogmatic Constitution on the Church," *The Documents of Vatican II*, ed. Walter Abbott, no. 48, pp. 78–79.

13. Gerard Manley Hopkins, "That Nature Is a Heraclitean Fire and of the Comfort of the Resurrection" in *The Complete Poems of Gerard Manley Hopkins* (New York: Oxford, 1948).

14. *The City of God*, Book XXII, p. 541.